What Others Are Saying About Positive Involvement:

"I am very enthusiastic about this book! It is clear, helpful, and will have a powerful impact on parents who want to help their kids learn. When we discuss the public school system in my graduate class, I use ideas from this book to help my students think about ways to improve children's learning."
—Dr. Robert D. Coursey, Professor of Psychology, University of Maryland

"We live in an age where learning the fundamentals of preparation for a successful life is obviously lacking. *Positive Involvement* is a very helpful tool for those who choose to accept the responsibility for their children and are willing to do it right. I commend the Youngbloods for their contribution."
—Congressman Zach Wamp, Third District, Tennessee

"This book is wonderful! As a grandparent, I feel it's an absolute necessity for parents. You can see yourself in it and what you would want to do. I wish I'd had this book years ago. I would like *my* children to read it!"
—Patricia Batson, grandmother and former teacher

"I totally agree with this approach. It makes sense. It works."
—Robert Love, Principal, St. Matthias School, Lanham, Maryland

"These days you read, over and over again, that parents need to be involved with their children's schoolwork. Seldom will you find a guide to that involvement as down to earth as this book. *Positive Involvement* contains concrete, practical suggestions that can apply to any parent, anywhere."
—Peggy Reiber, Headmistress, and Judy Smolen, Middle School Director, Holy Trinity Episcopal Day School, Bowie, Maryland

"*Positive Involvement* offers some of the best, most sensible solutions I've seen to the problems children and parents face with schoolwork. The key is commitment! If you are committed to helping your child, you'll find this book invaluable."
—Ronald Stuckey, Guidance Counselor,
Riverdale Baptist School, Upper Marlboro, Maryland

"The Youngbloods' research and personal experience confirm what I have observed during my career in education—that the role of the parent is key to the success of the child in the school setting. Parents and educators will appreciate the practical approach used to explain not just what needs to be done but how it needs to be accomplished."
—Dr. Gerald Boarman, Principal,
Eleanor Roosevelt High School, Greenbelt, Maryland

"In the speech President Kennedy was scheduled to give on that fateful day in Dallas, he would have said, 'There will always be . . . voices heard in the land, . . . finding fault, but never favor . . .' As parents, we want to find favor, not fault, with our children, as Jack and Marsha Youngblood's *Positive Involvement* emphasizes. This book is a treasure-house of information and inspiration. It should be read and re-read by every parent who cares."
—Congressman Andy Jacobs, Tenth District, Indiana

"This practical guide to parenting is sure to be a valuable resource of information and ideas for many parents. I commend the Youngbloods for taking the time to compile this wealth of knowledge and insights into young people in a format that is accessible and useful."
—Nancy Grasmick, Maryland Superintendent of Schools

"The Youngbloods have literally synthesized a world of experience into a user-friendly guide to help parents actively foster productive habits for their children."
—Dr. Harold E. Shinitzky, Faculty, Johns Hopkins University
School of Medicine, Department of Pediatrics

Positive Involvement

Positive
Involvement

How to Teach Your Child
Habits for School Success

Jack and Marsha Youngblood

The BrownWood Press

Positive Involvement: How to Teach Your Child Habits for School Success. Published 1995 in the United States of America by the BrownWood Press.

The BrownWood Press
7529 Greenbelt Road, Suite 105
Greenbelt, Maryland 20770-3403
(301) 345-8505

ORDERING INFORMATION
Individual sales. Additional copies of this book are available directly from the publisher at the address above.
Quantity sales. Special discounts are available on quantity purchases by schools, associations, and other groups. For details, contact the BrownWood Press.
Orders by U.S. trade bookstores and wholesalers. Please contact the publisher at the address above for trade terms.

Production supervised by Jenna Dixon
Copyedited by Linda Lotz   Proofread by Edith Sard
Text designed and typeset by Jenna Dixon
Index prepared by Barbara DeGennaro

Printed in the United States of America on recycled acid-free paper by Bookcrafters. Text printed with soy-based ink.

Publisher's Cataloging in Publication
Youngblood, Jack F.
    Positive involvement : how to teach your child habits for school success / Jack and Marsha Youngblood. – Greenbelt, MD : BrownWood Press, 1995.
        p.   cm.
    Includes bibliographic references and index.
    ISBN 0-9647295-0-4
    1. Education–Parent participation. 2. Study skills. 3. Child rearing.
I. Youngblood, Marsha. II. Title.
LB1049.Y68   1995
371.3'0281   QBI95-20342

04 03 02 01 00 99 98 97 96 95   10 9 8 7 6 5 4 3 2 1   1st Printing 1995

I had always thought that a nightingale's incomparable song was instinctive or inherited. But it is not so. . . . A "master bird" . . . daily sings its lovely song, and the infant bird listens for a period of about a month. In this way the little wild bird is trained by the master bird.

–Shinichi Suzuki
Nurtured by Love

Contents

Introduction

*Parents need to slow down their lives to help their children grow. . . .
Many parents and other family members are stretched to the limit −
juggling jobs, putting food on the table, getting their children to safe
after-school programs − doing all they can to keep body and soul
together. But I believe that we are missing something far deeper in
all this rushing around. . . . The education of American children −
their moral development, their sense of citizenship, and academic
growth − is done in fits and starts. This is not how families want to
raise their children.*

−Secretary of Education Richard Riley
Address at the National Press Club, 1994

At our first overseas school, an international school in
northern India, we taught with two teachers, Eleanor and
Ray Dunn, who knew the importance of helping their
fifth-grade son realize his natural talent. And they knew how to
guide him to success and self-confidence. Kevin was not a naturally great student in school: he loved working with his hands,
building things, tinkering. He was bright and capable, but he
didn't know how to translate his brightness into school success.

That's where his parents came in. They knew their son's
strengths but recognized that school rewards only certain kinds
of intelligence, that he might be frustrated and his self-image
seriously undermined if he had to do his work all alone. With
his parents' help, Kevin learned how to set regular times for
doing his schoolwork, how to keep track of assignments, how to
persevere and complete his work on time. At the time we knew

the Dunns, Kevin struggled in school, but he did all his work. He made good grades (B's), and his natural intelligence and enthusiasm remained undimmed. He was clearly competent and thus felt good about himself.

This is exactly what *Positive Involvement: How to Teach Your Child Habits for School Success* is about – how we parents can teach our children to do their schoolwork, how we can help them build skills, habits, and attitudes that will eventually lead to success in school – and in later life.

We called the Dunns at their home in Canada when we started to write this book to ask what had happened to Kevin during the last ten years. Eleanor told us that he had taken a combination of practical arts (shop, woodworking, and so on) and college preparatory courses in high school. He had made straight A's in all of them. Though his parents hadn't pressured him to make high grades, they came naturally with the skills and self-confidence he had built.

With his parents' encouragement, Kevin went on to a college with a strong vocational and trades emphasis, where he finished a diploma in architecture and contracting. Before he graduated, he was already in demand as a building contractor, doing occasional jobs in his last year of college. An employer told his parents, "You have a wonderful son – he always sticks to a job until it's done!" Kevin had a job waiting for him when he finished college.

Since coming back to the United States in 1991, we have met quite a few parents like the Dunns who know the importance of guiding their children through school as a preparation for life. Unlike the Dunns, many of these are single parents. We've included in this book a number of anecdotes about these families and their successes.

However, through our work tutoring and running study skills and SAT classes and parent workshops, we have found many more parents who want to help their children but don't know what to do. We've heard the same things over and over.

"All Brent wants to do is play sports, watch TV, play video games. I try to get him to work but can't even find out what his homework is."

"I'd like to help my son, but he won't let me. I can't get him to do any homework."

"My daughter used to make pretty good grades until she hit the seventh grade. Then she went down hill. She doesn't work now, isn't interested in school, and I can't seem to motivate her."

"Will makes terrible grades and he hates school. The other kids even pick on him a lot, or so he says. It's hard to get him to go to school, much less do the homework. Yet the school still passes him along each year. I don't know what to do."

"We thought Mary was doing fine this year when suddenly she brought home a report card with two D's and an F on it. She says she does her homework at school. She sure doesn't do it at home."

We've found that the first reaction of parents confronting these kinds of problems is to look outside the family for a solution, saying things like: "Let's look for a better school, or a better teacher. Let's hire a tutor. Let's put our child in a study skills class."

However, as you'll see in Chapter 1, there is another solution – one that's much more likely to yield results. That is for parents to become positively involved in their children's schoolwork. It doesn't matter whether both parents are working or whether there's only one parent in the home. It doesn't matter whether children are planning to go to vocational school, to college, or directly into the workforce when they graduate from high school. Positive parent involvement is still the answer that is most likely to yield results.

Although positive parent involvement is simple, it's not necessarily easy. It's not a quick fix. Being positively involved may mean a commitment of time and energy over a fairly long period of time. It may mean making some hard choices. It may mean parents' changing some of their habits and priorities.

In *The Read-Aloud Handbook*, Jim Trelease tells about a woman coming up to him following a PTA meeting where he had been discussing the benefits of reading aloud to children for a few minutes every day.[1] This mother told him that reading aloud every day was impossible in her home – she and her husband both worked and had little time left over. Trelease sympathized with her, saying that he and his wife had the same problem, and then he said: "And just when I think there isn't enough time to spare for the night's reading, I ask myself: Which is more precious – my time or my child? Which can I more easily afford to waste?"

As the woman walked away, Trelease wondered whether she really understood what happens during those few minutes a day we spend reading to our sons and daughters. He speaks of this time as building "bridges between parent and child." The same is true of time spent helping our children with their schoolwork – it's a way to build some bridges, an opportunity to be in touch with their lives.

Part I
Getting Started

- Parents Are the Key

- A Model for Positive Involvement

- Applying the Model to Schoolwork

Chapter 1
Parents Are the Key

Q: What has the greatest effect on a child's success in school?
    a. the money spent on education
    b. the quality of his teachers
    c. the involvement of his parents

Answer: c.

In the last 15 years, every major study on this topic has concluded that parents' involvement has more influence on children's success in school than the quality of the teachers or the school.
  –Bruce Baron, Christine Baron, and Bonnie MacDonald
      What Did You Learn in School Today?

What does it really take to be positively involved in your children's schooling? What does it take to make that difference? How do you sustain your involvement? Where do you start?

Pulitzer Prize–winning columnist William Raspberry wrote: "I suspect that the single biggest reason for noninvolvement is as simple as this: Parents don't know how important they are to their children's academic success, and they don't know what to do."[1]

Positive parent involvement begins by parents becoming 100 percent convinced that their involvement is important to their children's success.

A mother called to get help for her eighth-grade son, Casey. He had been diagnosed with a mild learning disorder, wasn't doing his homework, and had grades of C or below, with math as the lowest. A few days later, the father brought Casey in to the learning center for math tutoring. His father explained that even though he and Casey's mother were divorced, they had both agreed at the beginning of the fall semester to get involved with Casey's schoolwork. They were working with him on a regular basis. Arranging for tutoring was just one part of their involvement.

Casey proved quite willing to do his math work during the tutorials. We suspected that this was because his parents gave a good bit of attention to his schoolwork. Two months later, Casey switched from tutorials into the Kumon Math Program, which gives students daily math work at an easy level and moves them ahead at their own pace (see page 130).

Five weeks later, Casey's father said, "I can't tell you how happy I am. Now Casey does all his schoolwork along with the daily math worksheets, and all his grades are up."

During the conversation that followed, he explained, "I committed myself to working with him, and I sat down with Casey every day. To tell the truth, in the beginning, I did a lot of his schoolwork for him, and I wasn't happy about that. Now I don't have to sit with him. Once he formed the habit of working, everything else followed. He writes his assignments down and does them."

At the end of that third quarter, Casey's report card showed all B's except for a C in math. When the semester ended, Casey's father called to say that Casey had won the "most improved student" awards in science and math at his middle school.

Casey's improvement resulted from the daily work habits he developed because of his parents' concern and involvement. As his father said, "When Casey's mother and I decided to get involved and committed time to Casey's schoolwork, things began to change."

There's a message in that for all parents, and it's borne out by research. In preparing to write this book, we looked at over 100 studies on parent involvement in education. The message was clear: If you want your child to do well in school, get involved! Spend time every day. Give your attention to your child's work.

Researcher Anne Henderson summed up her survey of forty-eight studies on the subject this way:[2]

When parents are involved, children begin to achieve.

Specifically,

- children earn higher grades

- children score higher on standardized tests

- children show positive attitudes and behavior in school and at home

And the things parents do can be simple. Reginald Clark published a study of ten African American families who lived in the same Chicago housing development.[3] These inner-city families were alike in most ways – socially, economically – but different in that five of the families had children in the upper 20 percent of their senior class and five had children in the lower 20 percent. What accounted for this difference?

Clark found that the traditional things research points to – income level, mother's educational background, and number of parents in the home – did not account for this difference in the children's performance. In fact, three out of the five high achieving seniors came from single-parent homes. It was what the parents *did* with their children that made the difference.

The parents of the high performing students:

- talked frequently with the children

- strongly encouraged academic pursuits

- set clear limits in the home

- created a nurturing environment at home

- monitored how the children spent their time

These parents also held certain views about education: they believed that the children's job was to learn in school and that the parents' job was to help them learn.

These are the kinds of things that Secretary of Education Richard Riley was talking about when he said, "Research shows that all families, whatever their income or education level, can take concrete steps that significantly help children learn."[4]

Parent Attention Is Powerful

Researchers looking at 1,900 students in inner-city London illustrated the power of parent attention very well.[5] They randomly divided these children from lower-income and multi-ethnic families into three groups to see which group improved the most in reading.

- The control group did nothing extra – just regular schoolwork.

- The second group of children read aloud to their parents for half an hour two to four times a week. The parents received either instruction in how to listen well or just encouragement from the child's teacher.

- The third group of students worked two extra hours a week with a trained reading teacher. The teacher instructed them in reading and listened to these children read aloud.

The results were startling. The group that simply read to their parents improved far more than the other two groups. Those students showed "a highly significant improvement in reading level." Perhaps even more surprising, the students taught by a reading teacher improved no more than the control group – the ones who did nothing extra!

The researchers called this effect "ineffable," something they couldn't explain or identify, but that produced results. As we'll show later, parent attention is far from ineffable. It is at the heart of much of children's early learning and should be at the heart of their later work.

This research showed that parents were more effective than reading experts. But most of us would find this hard to believe because we aren't aware of the power of parents' positive attention. We're prone to think that the "experts" can do it better.

Two psychologists reported a parent saying something they had heard often: "Oh, you're a psychologist! My son will listen to you."

"Not true," these psychologists said. They explained that parents are the most effective people with their own children, especially if they have some understanding of their role – what to do and how to do it.[6]

Children Know the Power of Parent Attention

Surprisingly, children of all ages appear to know how important their parents' involvement in their schoolwork is, even if they don't readily admit it – especially as they grow older.

The National Association of Secondary School Principals and the Sylvan Learning Center surveyed more than 13,000 high school juniors and seniors all across the country in public, private, urban, and rural high schools.[7] They found that these students blamed their poor academic performance on the schools and on their parents, not on themselves or their teachers. Seventy-four percent of these students rated their parents as marginally to rarely involved with their schoolwork.

In other words, they recognized that they needed their parents' help to do well in school. And what kind of help did they want from their parents? The students said that they wanted "help with homework, educational opportunities outside of school, and home study rules" – some of the very things Reginald Clark found effective parents doing.

A recent survey of 1,300 ninth-grade students in six Maryland high schools found this same recognition of the importance of parents.[8] Eighty-two percent agreed that they needed their parents to be involved in their schoolwork. Fifty percent said that they wanted their parents to be more involved than they were. Over 75 percent of these high schoolers acknowledged that they would be willing to:

- ask a parent for help in studying for a test

- show a parent something he or she did well in school

- work with parents to improve grades

- ask parents for ideas for a story or project

Parents' Lack of Confidence in Their Role

Parents are not only important to their children's academic success, they are of key importance. Research shows it, and children know it. And parents want to help their children. Eighty percent of the parents surveyed in the Maryland high school study mentioned above said that they wanted to spend more time with their children on homework.[9] Ivy Lovelady, prominent for her work in urban and rural schools in Mississippi, believes that all parents would like to participate in their children's education. "Generally, the situation is one of parents not knowing *how* to get involved," she says.[10]

That's the second half of what William Raspberry called the biggest reason for parental noninvolvement: parents don't get involved "because they don't know what to do."[11] Seventy percent of the parents in the Maryland survey said that they wanted more information from the school on how they could best help their children with schoolwork.[12]

There's a good reason for that. Most of us have spent time doing things that don't work – nagging, doing work for children, pressuring them to get high grades at any cost, making them feel guilty, punishing them for low grades.

But as you'll see in the next chapter, all of us knew how to be positively involved when our children were infants. We've just forgotten.

Chapter 2
A Model for Positive Involvement

"Do you want to play some golf?" Moses asked Jesus.

When Moses named the course, Jesus asked, "Why that one?"

"It's Arnold Palmer's favorite," Moses replied. Jesus agreed to go along.

On the third tee Moses pulled out a five iron to hit over the water hazard. "You ought to use a wood," Jesus suggested." You'll never clear the water with that."

As he hit the ball, Moses replied, "Arnold Palmer always plays a five iron on this tee." The ball landed in the middle of the pond.

Walking out across the water, Jesus retrieved the ball, handed it back to Moses and said, "You really should try your three wood."

"Nope," Moses insisted. "Arnold Palmer always uses a five iron. If it's good enough for him, it's good enough for me." He hit the ball into the pond again.

This time Moses went to get the ball. Parting the waters, he walked out on the dry pond bottom.

A man, who was now waiting to play the same hole, couldn't believe his eyes. "Who does that guy think he is? Moses?"

"No, " Jesus replied, "unfortunately, he thinks he's Arnold Palmer."

Moses was a prophet. He could perform miracles. But when he tried to be something he was not – a professional golfer – he didn't do so well. Parents can't perform miracles, but they can do some amazing things in motivating their children to work and learn. To do that, though, they have to understand who they are and what their role is.

The problem is that when our children enter school, all of us tend to take on "schoolish" approaches to their efforts. We abandon the methods we used when they were infants, but those early methods actually contain the secret to positive involvement.

Indeed, virtually all parents have been positively involved in their children's learning. *You've done it all before* – when you helped your child learn to walk, talk, and function socially. Look at what happens in those early years.

Early Learning

Children learn wonderfully in their first four to five years. They learn to walk, talk, dress, feed themselves, and interact in their culture. This is no small thing.

A number of linguists have commented on how complex a task it is just to learn to speak a language fluently. This task includes:

- mastering a complete grammatical system so that the words come in the right order with the right endings

- mastering pronunciation of hundreds of words with the proper accent

- choosing the right word to convey a particular meaning

All these things children learn by the time they're five years old.

Shinichi Suzuki based his famous method for teaching young children to play the violin on children's early learning of language. In his book *Nurtured by Love*, he describes how he discovered his method:

> One day when we were practicing [violin] at the house of my younger brother, it hit me like a flash: all Japanese children speak Japanese! . . . Since they all speak Japanese so easily and fluently, there must be a secret; and this must be training.

Indeed, all children everywhere in the world are brought up by a perfect educational method: their mother tongue. Why not apply this method to other faculties? I felt I had made a tremendous discovery.[1]

Many educators and psychologists have noted the great learning that happens in those early years. Dr. Benjamin Bloom, considered by many to be the foremost educational theorist alive, studied this early learning in over 1,000 children. He concluded that by the time they are four, children have developed half of the intelligence they will have in their entire lives.[2]

Much of the reason for this growth is developmental. Children are like sponges in these early years, their brains expanding and growing at an incredible rate. There is no doubt that they are ready to learn and develop then.

At the same time that children are doing some incredible learning, parents are doing some marvelous teaching. They are teaching in a helpful, positive way. In fact, if we look at what parents do in those early years, we might have a model for positive involvement.

Early Teaching

Think back to what you did when you taught your child to walk. Kenneth Blanchard and Spencer Johnson give a great description of this in *The One Minute Manager*:

How do you think you teach them to walk? Can you imagine standing a child up and saying "Walk," and when he falls down you pick him up and spank him and say, "I told you to walk"? No, you stand the child up and the first day he wobbles a little bit, and you get all excited and say, "He stood, he stood," and you hug and kiss the child. The next day he stands for a moment and maybe wobbles a step and you are all over him with kisses and hugs. Finally, the child, realizing that this is a pretty good deal, starts to wobble his legs more and more until he eventually walks.[3]

The One Minute Manager also describes the process of learning to talk:

> Suppose you wanted a child to say, "Give me a glass of water, please." If you waited until the child said the whole sentence before you gave her any water, the child would die of thirst. So you start off by saying, "Water, water." All of a sudden one day the child says, "Waller." You jump all over the place, hug and kiss the child, get grandmother on the phone so the child can say, "Waller, waller." That wasn't water, but it was close.
>
> Now you don't want a kid going into a restaurant at the age of twenty-one asking for a glass of "waller" so after a while you only accept the word "water" and then you begin on "please."[4]

Look at these descriptions, and you'll see several things parents do that are helpful, effective, and even right in terms of learning theory.

Encouraging Effort

Parents know that when children try again and again, they'll eventually learn. So the parents' whole approach is to *encourage the child to make repeated efforts*. They do this in several ways:

1. Parents give the child's efforts their attention and enthusiasm, and this attention is completely positive.

2. Parents get excited over the child's slightest progress — "He said, 'waller,' did you hear that?" or "He stood! He stood!" They show their delight in their hugs and kisses and in telling grandmother — and everyone else — about their child's progress.

3. Parents also encourage repeated efforts by ignoring the child's unsuccessful attempts to walk and talk. Because they're only concerned that the child try, they are able to ignore "failures" and focus on the smallest bit of

progress. They don't even view these attempts as failures but as necessary steps toward the goal of learning to walk and talk, so failed attempts eventually become successes.

When parents encourage their children's efforts in this way, they are practicing two basic elements of educational psychology – *reinforcement* and *extinction of behavior*. Parents reinforce the behavior they want by giving it their attention. Specifically, they encourage the child to try over and over to walk or talk by giving these efforts great importance and their full attention. Second, they go bananas when the child shows the slightest progress. (They are "all over the kid with hugs and kisses.")

Parents make extinct the behavior they don't want by giving it no attention. They give no importance to any kind of failure. When the child tries to walk and falls, her mom picks her up and says, "Let's try that again." In fact, parents see the "failures" as necessary steps to actually succeeding, for that's what they truly are.

By giving failure no attention, they allow the child to give it no importance. Because parents ignore unsuccessful attempts to walk, the child is able to forget all her unsuccessful tries and remember only the successful ones.

Holding a Long-Term View

There's another aspect of parents' teaching a child to walk and talk that is more subtle, less obvious than encouraging the child's efforts. *They have a vision of where the child is going.* They know what they want their child to learn, and they also know that virtually all children will be successful.

First, parents have clear goals for their children. For example, they know that they eventually want their child to say, "Give me a glass of water, please." They want the child to walk and eventually run.

Second, *they expect success!* This one element underlies the others. It's at the heart of the matter. They're not concerned that the child can't say the entire sentence or can't walk right away because they know that the child will ultimately succeed.

How is it that parents are willing to try to teach their children to walk or talk? They don't get any special training. They don't take any college or even high school courses in teaching walking. Why are they willing to take this teaching on? They can do it because they know that all children learn these things in this way. They know that all parents teach their children to walk and talk, and they know that virtually all children are successful.

To sum up, this is what parents do:

Hold a vision by

- having clear goals
- expecting success

Encourage repeated efforts by

- giving full attention to efforts
- ignoring failures
- celebrating progress

This is a great starting point or model for positive parent involvement in schoolwork and for getting children to work hard.

Recognizing That Schoolwork Is More Complicated

"Wait a minute," you say, "doing schoolwork and learning to walk are not the same. It's not that simple when kids get older and enter school." You're right! Schoolwork is different. It's a different time, and what children are learning is more complicated. They are more complicated.

In school, children are no longer learning in a protected home environment. They are learning from strangers in the presence of strangers. They are performing in a place where their performance and even their efforts are being scrutinized, judged, weighed.

The parents' situation is different too. Their early involvement was spontaneous, unplanned, and instinctive. Involvement with studies must be more conscious, planned, and sustained to be effective.

These conditions make encouraging children's efforts that much more important. Children still need the same support parents gave them when they were small. They need someone to encourage them to try over and over again until they get it right . . . someone to give them their full, positive attention . . . someone to believe in them . . . someone to ignore their unsuccessful attempts . . . someone to see where they're going and inspire them to make more efforts.

What parents did in encouraging their children's efforts in learning to walk and talk is exactly what children need as they enter and progress through school. This is the parents' unique role. We can't expect schools to do all these things. It's important to understand this.

Here are three key things parents do that we can't expect from schools:

1. *Parents give their children's efforts their full, undivided attention.* Obviously, schools can't do this. Each teacher has many other children to attend to and cannot possibly give undivided attention to each child's efforts. And, of course, when the child does homework, the teacher isn't around.

2. *Parents expect their children will be 100 percent successful. There's no timetable for results, no pressure to learn by a certain time.* Schools can't operate like this. There are timetables, and teachers have to judge performance constantly. Schools expect that some children will succeed, some

will be less successful, and some will fail. These expectations are built into our grading system, into our standardized tests, into our labeling of children – gifted, average, talented, learning disabled. This isn't intended as an attack on schools. It's just important to see that parents' expectations are quite different, or at least they can be.

3. *Parents ignore the less successful attempts their children make and celebrate the more successful ones.* Parents know that children will learn by trying over and over again, so they don't give "failed" attempts much importance. Schools, of course, do not ignore unsuccessful attempts at learning, at least not for long. They do try to encourage students to make efforts, but then they have to turn around and judge these efforts.

Over many years of teaching, both of us have often felt as if we were constantly changing "hats." First we wore the "white hat" and took the role of encouraging kids to make efforts, to try hard. As teachers, that usually felt pretty good. But then we had to put on the "black hat" to judge and grade those efforts. That often felt terrible to us and to the kids. This is one aspect of teaching that many teachers have trouble with as an experience of Marsha's illustrates.

Marsha taught in a special program preparing minority students to enter college. One of the students had very poor writing skills, but with Marsha's direction and encouragement, she worked hard at writing for an entire quarter. She wrote four or five papers focusing on skills in organizing her ideas and in combining sentences so her ideas would flow. The girl progressed, and her writing improved, but it usually fell far short of the standard required for the course or for college. On her final project, she was able to produce a good, solid C paper. That was the grade she deserved. It was an honest grade and reflected a good improvement. But to the student, it was not enough.

After getting her grade, the girl sought Marsha out. "You encouraged me and showed me what to do. And I did what you told me to," she said. "But after all my work, you gave me a C. What's the point of working if this is what I get?" And the girl turned and walked away.

Marsha still remembers that terrible feeling of being caught between two roles – one minute encouraging a student to work hard and the next minute having to judge her efforts. She knew that if the student had been able and willing to sustain her work over a longer period of time, she would have eventually produced better writing that deserved a higher grade. But it wasn't possible to show the girl that.

This is where parents come in. Parents have to play only one role. They can encourage children to make efforts with no concern for results. They can free children to make efforts unclouded by fear of failure. This is the parents' unique role, and it's the essence of motivation.

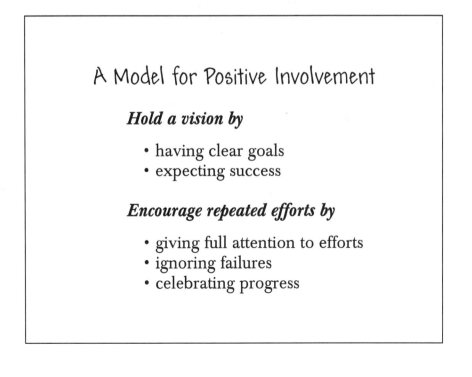

A Model for Positive Involvement

Hold a vision by

- having clear goals
- expecting success

Encourage repeated efforts by

- giving full attention to efforts
- ignoring failures
- celebrating progress

Chapter 3
Applying the Model to Schoolwork

Every single human being's personality – his ability, his way of thinking and feeling – is carved and chiseled by training and environment. It shows in each person's face and eyes. His whole character becomes visible. The stamp of history changes day by day, matching the steps of man's living. This is life's delicate working.
—Shinichi Suzuki
Nurtured by Love

When our own daughter Sarah started kindergarten, we hadn't thought much about our role in school. In fact, we hadn't really planned to be involved. Like many parents, we just assumed that it was the school's job to teach her, and that was that! But our daughter's first experiences in school changed our minds, and we struggled to learn what to do.

We were moving from teaching in an international school in the Himalayan Mountains of India to a U.S. State Department school in Saudi Arabia. Because of a serious delay in our visas, we arrived two months after school had started.

Our daughter hadn't yet started to read, unlike many of her classmates. We had believed that building a strong interest in reading through reading aloud with her would be enough. School would do the rest, or so we thought. We didn't realize that reading was a big part of the kindergarten curriculum at our new school.

Because she arrived two months late and hadn't begun to read, Sarah was placed in the "redbird" reading group for slow or beginning readers. The fast readers were called the "blue-birds." Unfortunately, the children came to believe that one group was "smart" and the other "dumb." The next fall when she entered first grade, this belief was strengthened. Students from the higher reading groups were selected for the school's gifted and talented enrichment program, and students from other reading groups were not.

Around the middle of the fall semester of our daughter's first-grade year, we realized that there was a serious problem. She didn't like going to school. There were tears for one reason or another almost every morning before school. But more important, from things she said, we could see that our daughter was beginning to see herself in unhelpful ways. She felt that she was not bright and capable.

During Christmas vacation of that first-grade year, we finally accepted that she needed help with reading. Neither of us was an elementary teacher, but we consulted some friends and bought a good series of short, highly simplified fairy tales. We began to read these with her over Christmas vacation: we read to her, and she read to us. Her favorite one was *The Elves and the Shoe-maker* – she must have read it a hundred times!

After the vacation we continued reading with her every night, and her reading progressed quickly. She continued to improve through first grade. By second grade she was reading so well that she plunged into *Little House on the Prairie*, a book series normally recommended for grades three through five. She read the entire set.

Her feelings about school and herself were slow to change, however. We knew that Sarah was bright and capable, but she didn't seem to know it. We weren't sure what to do to help her believe in herself.

We thought that making higher grades might help, so we pressed her – gently, we thought – for results. But the high grades didn't come consistently, and somehow we managed to communicate a certain disappointment in her school performance. We weren't happy with this situation, but we weren't sure what we wanted out of school for our daughter. We certainly didn't want her to be miserable – after all, she had to spend thirteen years of her life there. We knew that those years would leave their mark – positive or negative.

Researchers have discovered and labeled two parenting styles that don't work – authoritarian and permissive.[1] During Sarah's early years in school, we became adept at both, going back and forth between them. We would ignore her schoolwork (permissive) until we thought there was a problem. If she wasn't doing as well as we thought she should, we would press her for better results and control her study time (authoritarian). When we realized that we had gone too far and had become too authoritarian, we would pull back again to being permissive. In this way we vacillated between two ineffective parenting styles. But we couldn't see a way out.

Getting a Perspective on School

In 1985, when our daughter entered the third grade, we once again changed schools and countries to teach at the Karachi American School in Pakistan. Early that year, our superintendent, David Chojnacki, said something in a faculty meeting that gave us a way to get a perspective on school and our role in it. He stopped a heated debate on after-school activities with remarks that went something like this:

"We could talk on and on about whether we need to offer one more activity or one less activity of any type. But we need to deal with a more basic issue first. I want to suggest an exercise for you that I've tried and found useful. It's a way to develop a more detached perspective on school and on our role in it. Please imagine that it's graduation, and all the students are leaving. Ask yourself this question: What kind of person do we want walking out of this school at graduation? What qualities, values, habits, and habitual ways of thinking would you wish for that student?"

This exercise was startling for us as teachers. We weren't used to thinking of what we wanted for our students beyond academics, beyond sports, beyond this week, this term. But it was even more startling for us as parents. This is what we had been looking for – a way to get a long-term perspective on our daughter. We began to ask ourselves: *What kind of person do we want walking out of our house in three, five, ten years? What values, habits, and attitudes do we want her to have? How can her school experience help her become that person?*

Later that evening we talked about David's question and our goals and wishes for our daughter. We realized that we didn't really have any long-term goals beyond vaguely wanting her to do well and be happy. But we decided that we should come up with some clear, simple ideas to serve as a guide, to give us a perspective. When we made our first list, it looked something like this. We wanted our daughter to:

- be a good, kind, loving person

- be competent and confident in schoolwork

- learn to work hard

- do her best and persevere in whatever she is given to do

- learn to read, write, and do math well

Getting Back to Encouraging Effort

It hit us that grades weren't that important in what we wanted for our daughter. They weren't even on our list. We came to see that a long-term perspective would allow us to relax our concerns about immediate results. It would enable us to get back to the kind of positive involvement we had enjoyed when our daughter was a baby. We hadn't been so concerned with results then because we knew that they would come if she just put in regular effort.

Our role now would be to encourage her efforts and support them. We saw that if we gave her schoolwork our attention and made the work – not grades – a real priority, our daughter would develop the ability to do her assignments every day. Once that hard work became a habit, other qualities would follow automatically – becoming skilled at learning, becoming confident.

Over time, we saw that our work was simple and remarkably like the role we played when our daughter learned to walk and talk – encouraging effort, giving that effort our attention, and giving little or no attention to negative results or what looked like failures. Having a long-term perspective made it relatively easy to do this. And it made it easy to be "tough," to insist that schoolwork come first, when necessary. We could be firm about making efforts, not about results.

Well, no bells went off, no miracles happened in the beginning. But we were very clear now about what we wanted from our daughter in school, and we knew what our role was in helping her. We knew or expected that she would gradually become competent in her subjects just by doing her work, and we hoped that in time she would become confident about her ability. We also believed that even the grades would eventually come for her.

Taking this long-term approach was also good for us. It enabled us to be involved with her life positively. Because we got back to encouraging her efforts in school without a lot of concern for the short-term results, we could relax and enjoy our daughter's development. At the very least, it let us get out of the way of her development.

As for her performance in school, we're not suggesting that there was a cause-and-effect relationship to the changes in our parenting, but she has succeeded beyond our expectations. Over several years, Sarah developed the habit of working, of doing each day's work well and thoroughly. Out of that habit came skill and comfort with schoolwork. By ninth grade, she began to excel, becoming a straight A student and excelling in sports (running) and music (flute.) More recently, we've found ourselves in the role of advising her not to work too hard, to lighten up.

But she has learned habits and attitudes that will last her for life. Most important, she finally sees herself as the bright and capable person she is, and she has that basic confidence that comes from much success.

To sum up, positive involvement allows parents to get back into the role they played when their children were young. Here is the model for positive parent involvement from Chapter 2 – adapted to schoolwork.

A Model for Positive Involvement with Schoolwork

Getting a vision

- Set long-term goals
- Know that hard work leads to success
- Believe in your child

Encouraging efforts

- Understand that habit is the key to motivation
- Establish the homework habit
    - Give homework positive attention
    - Ignore failures
    - Celebrate progress

Part II
Getting a Vision

- Setting Goals

- Hard Work Leads to Success

- Believing in Your Child

Chapter 4
Setting Goals

"Living backward!" Alice repeated in great astonishment. "I never heard of such a thing!"

"—but there's one great advantage in it, that one's memory works both ways."

"I'm sure mine only works one way," Alice remarked. "I can't remember things before they happen."

"It's a poor sort of memory that only works backward," the Queen remarked.

"What sort of things do you remember best?" Alice ventured to ask.

"Oh, the things that happen the week after next," the Queen replied.

                                    —Lewis Carroll
                            Through the Looking Glass

In the last chapter, we talked about the question that helped us get a better picture of what we wanted for our daughter: *What kind of person/student do I want my child to become?* That is, what qualities, attitudes, and habits would I wish for my child?

Since returning to the United States, we've asked this question of parents from different racial and religious backgrounds, parents from different economic and social backgrounds, and single parents of both sexes. We wanted to see whether their answers had anything in common.

One woman with two sons laughed and said, "I want them to be brilliant and popular . . . to make straight A's and to be the stars of their class." But then she said, "Let me think about it, and discuss it with my husband." A few days later she handed us a list that included: "They should be independent and practical. I want them to be able to get things done, to know their strengths and be confident." Like other parents we spoke with, when she thought more deeply about this question, she switched from results-oriented goals to ones with more depth — qualities, attitudes, and habits she wanted her sons to develop.

It wasn't a new question to some good friends of ours, Carolyn and Chuck Johnson. They had thought about this issue for several years and gave a well-thought-out list of answers.

They wanted their children to:

1. Want to learn

2. Have the skills to learn
     to read
     to be organized
     to be able to concentrate
     to solve problems

3. Be able to persevere in working

4. Have the desire to achieve

5. Have confidence
     to be their own persons, have faith in themselves
     to believe they can achieve
     to make choices
     to stand up for themselves or someone else
     to do the right thing

6. Be decent people

7. Recognize their obligations; accept responsibility

8. Be brave enough to take risks

9. Know their own strengths and weaknesses

10. Be able to work past frustration

In answering this question, most parents didn't give such point-by-point, highly organized answers. Many of the goals or qualities parents identified were similar to the ones we had identified. And yes, the parents agreed on many goals for their children, despite the diversity of their backgrounds.

Some of the goals they came up with may not seem to relate directly to doing schoolwork – for example, wanting a child to be a decent person and to be comfortable relating to people. However, many of the qualities the parents agreed on clearly come out of and relate to schoolwork. On the following page we list our own main headings and then give parents' exact words under each heading.

This exercise helped us gain a perspective on our daughter's schoolwork. It allowed us to pull back from the goals and perspectives that schools promote and to move toward a positive involvement in schoolwork – toward encouraging effort and ignoring failure. It helped us make our peace with grades, to get over being too concerned with them. In fact, it helped us begin to ignore them.

Why Grades Make Terrible Goals

Grades are the chief motivators used by most schools – they are themselves rewards and punishments. If students get A's, they will "make" the honor roll or the principal's list. The parents attend honors ceremonies and teas. The children receive ribbons and awards. However, students who earn D's or F's make a different principal's list. They get invited to extra meetings after class. Their parents are invited to conferences to hear the bad news and consider ways to improve their children's performance.

Why are grades terrible goals? The first reason is that high grades require sustained effort over a long time. Grades come out every nine weeks or so. To get good grades, students have to make consistent efforts over those nine weeks – doing all homework assignments, studying for quizzes and tests, writing

Results from Parent Survey

I want my children to:

1. Have confidence, faith in themselves
    "Be brave enough to take risks"
    "Not be afraid to take risks"
    "Think for themselves and stand up for
      themselves or for someone else"
    "Be able to hold on to their own value base
      and culture"
    "Be independent"

2. Have the skills to learn
    "Be able to read, solve problems"
    "Be able to concentrate"
    "Get as much education as needed for jobs"
    "Be well-grounded in academics"

3. Learn the value of hard work
    "Complete tasks"
    "Get things done"
    "Get the job done"
    "Be able to work past frustration"
    "Be disciplined"
    "Develop work habits that will help them in
      the job world"
    "Persevere until a job is done"

papers, doing long-term projects. The truth is, most kids are not used to working hard enough and long enough to do it.

Letty Rosen, dean of students for grades five through eight at Newport School in Kensington, Maryland, knew this very well. In 1991, she explained why she was considering offering some middle school study skills classes: "The kids start the year fresh and enthusiastic at being in school with a clean slate. They come back wanting to do well, to do all their work, and make great grades. But that enthusiasm goes after only a couple of weeks of school for some, a month for others – when they've missed a few assignments, not done well on a test or quiz, gotten a few low grades, then their resolve to work hard disappears. I want some workshops from an outsider as a way to keep up their interest and enthusiasm."

When grades don't come easily, most kids, as Letty said, give up their efforts. This is not surprising. Students are usually shooting for A's. After a few weeks, when they start getting back papers with B's, C's, and D's on them, they know that their target of an A is out of range. What happens? Their resolve to put in effort at schoolwork slackens. "What's the point?" they say, "I'll never get an A now." They may even give up completely and stop working altogether.

The second reason that grades make terrible goals is that it takes time for children to learn how to do what is needed to earn high grades. It takes time to develop the habits and skills required – and children need support and guidance to make an effort every day.

Probably the biggest single mistake parents make with schoolwork is emphasizing grades and results without giving this support.

Why Hard Work Is a Better Goal

If you think back to when you taught your children to walk and talk, you'll remember that you didn't emphasize results. In fact, you ignored all the unsuccessful attempts the child made. Why? Because you knew that if the child kept trying, she would be successful. All you cared about was that she keep trying. You weren't concerned about when she could actually walk – and eventually run. You knew it would take a long time. You regarded each step toward learning to walk as part of the child's final success in walking.

That's exactly the approach to take with children's school-work. You don't want to focus on results, on grades. You want to focus instead on children's making efforts, just as they did in walking and talking. You want to give those efforts your attention and your encouragement.

And what are these efforts in school? It's children doing their work every day. So one of the important shifts in thinking we need to make is to realize that *our goal is not grades, not performance, but efforts.* The goal is to get children to work hard. That's the effort parents want to encourage in school.

If you look back at the long-term goals common to the parents we polled, one is to "learn the value of hard work." This includes completing tasks, persevering to finish a job, learning to do a job thoroughly and well, putting in 100 percent effort. Actually, the goal of getting your child to work hard includes all these things. If you think about it, children will achieve most other goals if they achieve this one goal. Out of working hard come the skills and habits to do the work.

Consider, for instance, what comes out of making 100 percent effort. Colman McCarthy wrote about an experiment he tried in a high school class in the Washington, D.C. area.[1] As the students prepared to turn in the papers he'd assigned them two weeks earlier, McCarthy made an unusual request. He asked the students to write on the cover page of their papers the percentage of effort they had exerted on the assignment – and to be truthful. Startled because no one had ever asked them to do this before, the students estimated their effort.

This is what McCarthy found when he read the papers: Only three students out of a class of thirty said that they had put in

100 percent effort. Most admitted to somewhere between full effort (100 percent) and halfhearted effort (50 percent).

When he returned these papers several days later, he reported to the class that "the 100 percent papers reflected fullness of effort" – well-argued points and concise, lively language. Students then tried to justify their lack of effort – noisy roommates, after-school jobs, and the clincher, "80 percent effort is good enough."

McCarthy countered with: "After high school or college, job-seeking time, will you tell the interviewer you're eager to work but you'll be giving only 80 percent effort? In school, did you go out for a varsity sport and tell the coach you'd give 50 percent effort?"

When children put in regular, 100 percent effort in school, they gain many things, including what McCarthy calls "the deepest joy in life" – giving your best to something. Out of this will eventually come results in many forms. They will develop skills in reading, writing, math, social studies, and science. They will learn to prepare tasks, to pace themselves in doing their work, to balance the different tasks they have to do. Many of these things are on the lists of the parents we interviewed. They may be on your list too.

Even grades will eventually come from reaching this one goal. As one mother told her daughter after they had heard this model for positive involvement: "If you do your work every day like that, you'll get good grades." That's right. If children keep on doing their work, day in and day out, the results, the grades, will eventually come. Sustained effort is what's required.

So, as parents wanting to be positively involved in schoolwork, our work starts by knowing where we are going, by having a clear vision of what we want our children to gain from the school experience. We start by asking and seriously answering the question:

What kind of person/student do I want my child to become?

It's a useful exercise. You may want to do it now. Use the worksheet on the next page.

Last year we met a parent who knew how much involvement it takes to lead children to work hard. Her son was enrolled in a study skills–speed reading class at a private school in Maryland.

When Martin came into the first class, the other students were surprised. "You're an A student," they said. "Why are you in this class?"

Martin was self-confident and comfortable enough with himself to say, "I'm here because I want to improve my reading."

Some weeks later, Martin's mother attended the parents' part of the study skills class, a workshop on positive involvement. After the parent session, his mother explained that she was involved with Martin most nights – sometimes for two or three hours. She didn't do his work for him – that would be easy and quick. Making sure that a student does his or her own work well can be time-consuming. She did whatever it took to make sure that Martin knew how to do his homework and did it well, and that took time.

What she said next showed that she had a vision: "Sometimes I come home from my job quite tired. But I don't mind spending the time with Martin on his schoolwork because *I know what it will do for him.* I know how valuable it is for him to learn these habits."

Worksheet for Setting Goals

What habits do I want my child to have in three, five, ten years?

_____

_____

_____

What attitudes do I want my child to hold?

_____

_____

_____

What qualities would I wish my child to develop?

_____

_____

_____

Chapter 5
Hard Work Leads
to Success

The child who "made it" was not always the one who was considered to be the most "talented." . . . The characteristic that distinguished the high achiever in the field from his or her siblings, most parents said, was a willingness to work and a desire to excel.

—Benjamin Bloom
Developing Talent in Young People

. . . over the last 30 years, parents, politicians, educators . . . have given kids license to put as little effort as possible into their education. And I'm not talking primarily about low-income minority kids who are allowed to graduate from our high schools reading and computing on a fifth-grade level, but about kids with solid SAT's who are going to the best colleges in the country.

—Patrick Welsh
"Classroom Potatoes"

As parents, we know that children succeed in walking and talking by making repeated efforts, so it's easy to encourage those efforts. If we're going to support our children's efforts in school, we need to be convinced of the value of hard work. We need to know that they will succeed there also by making repeated efforts. Unfortunately, strong evidence exists that most Americans don't really believe that hard work is the basis for achievement in school.

Our daughter's chorus was asked to perform for her school's 1992 commencement ceremonies. As we waited to pick her up afterwards, we couldn't help overhearing two women's conversation.

"I thought the valedictorian gave a great address," one woman said. "She even seemed comfortable speaking to that huge crowd."

The second woman answered as they walked away, "Yeah, that girl has a whole lot of talent."

We were struck by what the second woman said, for it dramatized the attitudes many American parents and students hold: that ability or talent, not hard work, is the key to achievement in learning.

This raises an essential question, one parents need to answer before they can even begin to help and guide children in their schoolwork. What is responsible for achievement in learning, success in school?

What the Experts Say

One of the best known teachers in the United States is a man named Jaime Escalante. If you've seen the movie *Stand and Deliver*, you know why Escalante is famous: in the 1970s he created what was arguably the most successful Advanced Placement (AP) calculus program in the United States.

The students Escalante worked with at Garfield High School in East Los Angeles were mainly low-income Hispanics. In the year before Escalante's calculus program arrived at Garfield, the students there took a total of only ten AP exams to gain college credit. By 1989 "the school set a record with over 450 A.P. tests" taken in sixteen subjects in one year. More than fifty students took the most difficult AP test – the one in calculus. For over fifteen years Escalante's program at Garfield High School accounted for 25 to 30 percent of all Hispanics nationally taking this test.[1]

The program's success rate was equally phenomenal. In a period of ten years, 500 inner-city high school students at Garfield passed this exam. That's an average of fifty students a year.[2]

So what did Jaime Escalante do? What was the secret of his success? Did he think and speak in terms of talent and ability? Not at all. In fact, in an article written in 1990 about his program, Escalante said: "The key to my success with minority students is a very simple, time-honored tradition: hard work and lots of it."[3]

Just to join the Escalante Math Program, the students at Garfield had to make a commitment to working. They signed a contract promising to complete all daily homework, participate in Saturday morning and after-school study sessions, and attend summer programs at East Los Angeles College. Every morning before school, from 7 A.M., and every afternoon after school, until 6 P.M., those students could be seen at the school, hard at work. And Escalante was there with them. Sometimes in the role of teacher, sometimes cheerleader, other times dad. He modeled the hard work and commitment his students needed to succeed − and he demanded it from them.

If you think about it, hard work is the key to success in most areas of life.

In the early 1980s, Benjamin Bloom, renowned educational researcher at the University of Chicago, began a study to answer the question of what makes for achievement.[4] For this study, Bloom and some fellow researchers chose 120 of the most accomplished young Americans they could find, people who had achieved the highest levels of performance in their respective areas. These people included concert pianists, Olympic swimmers, research neurologists, mathematicians, tennis champions, and award-winning sculptors. The researchers studied these young people and their upbringing to see what they had in common that might account for their high achievement.

When you think of people who perform at such a high level, what do you credit their achievement to? Probably most of us would say talent or innate ability, just as the woman talking about the valedictorian spoke of her skill and competence in terms of talent.

But that's not what Bloom and his team of researchers found to be true. Bloom writes, "The child who 'made it' was not always the one who was considered to be the most 'talented.' Many parents described another one of their children as having more 'natural ability.' The characteristic that distinguished the high achiever in the field from his or her siblings, most parents said, was a willingness to work and a desire to excel. *Persistence*, *competitiveness*, and *eagerness* were other often-used terms."[5]

The researchers also discovered similarities in the home environments of those outstanding mathematicians, scientists, athletes, and artists.[6] Though their parents came from a variety of social and economic backgrounds, the parents were alike in two important things they did. One, they valued and modeled hard work, perseverance, and the desire to do a job well. Two, they showed their children that it wasn't their natural "ability" but what they did with it that mattered. In short, by their belief and example, the parents instilled in their children the value of hard work.

So, to the question of what makes for achievement, Bloom's book *Developing Talent in Young People* gives virtually the same answer as Jaime Escalante – that achievement comes from hard work. It's a simple notion, but one that is not so easy for many of us to accept.

The Overemphasis on Ability

When it comes to school learning, there is strong evidence that most Americans hold a different view from that of Escalante and Bloom – the view that ability, not hard work, is the key to achievement.

Harold Stevenson and James Stigler show this convincingly in *The Learning Gap*, a book about their eight-year study comparing schoolchildren in the United States, China, Taiwan, and Japan.[7] *The Learning Gap* goes beyond merely showing differences in performance, to identifying attitudes and beliefs that may well *cause* those differences. One of those is the American belief that ability is central to learning.

The study found that American mothers gave far more importance to ability than Chinese and Japanese mothers did, and that the children from each group reflected their mothers' attitudes and beliefs. For example, early in their schooling, the American children said that they believed that standardized tests could show how much ability they had. That wasn't true of the Asian children. They didn't view standardized test scores as signs of ability at all. To them, low test scores showed what students hadn't yet learned but would be able to learn through effort. High test scores showed that students had worked hard and learned a great deal.

This difference in belief is important for one reason: *hard work is something within our control,* whereas ability, or what we call ability, is not.

In a separate study,[8] Stevenson found similar differences in attitude among high school students when he asked eleventh-grade Asians and Americans to rank the most important factors in math performance. The Americans tended to give "a good teacher" a high ranking and "studying hard" one of the lowest. The Asians ranked "studying hard" as the most important factor and "a good teacher" as one of the least important. Stevenson comments that Americans favor effortlessness − reliance on the teacher, reliance on ability − whereas Asians favor working hard.

Where is all this leading? What is the point? In *The Learning Gap,* Stevenson and Stigler draw a startling conclusion: *an overemphasis on ability undercuts the efforts of all students.*[9]

This is a danger of the prevailing emphasis on testing. If we as parents give testing too much credence, then what's the point of effort? The researchers found that when we overemphasize ability, youngsters who get low test scores stop trying in school. They naturally come to feel that trying hard is useless − that it won't help them.

But they are not the only ones harmed. Those who get high scores on standardized tests also lose. If ability is the goal, and they have ability, what's left for them to do? These students come to believe that they don't *need* to work hard in school. They often apply themselves less in school, and their performance suffers. We saw an illustration of this in 1987, when we were teaching at the Karachi American School.

A boy in Jack's seventh-grade math class had been selected for the Talent Identification Program, a summer "gifted and talented" program at Duke University. The sole basis for selection into this program is a high score on the Scholastic Assessment Test (SAT), a test widely used for college admission. After his selection, both he and his mother were understandably happy and proud. But then a disturbing thing happened: the boy's performance in math and several other subjects declined dramatically because he stopped doing regular homework, and he seemed to stop studying for tests.

During a meeting with teachers to discuss her son's lower grades, his mother said: "I can't understand his poor performance. Just look at his SAT scores. You can see how smart he is." The mother blamed the school, and she blamed the teachers for her son's decline. "He's bored," she charged. "You don't interest him in his subjects. Then you give him low grades."

This mother just couldn't see that despite high SAT scores, the boy needed to do his work. He needed to master the material. Then he would not only earn high grades but also develop his abilities and perhaps even feel good about himself and the work he had accomplished. It was clear that his SAT scores and his selection for Duke's program had undercut his willingness to work.

Almost All Children Have Enough "Talent"

Not only do we give too much importance to ability, but we *think* that there are greater differences in people's ability to learn than there actually are. This emphasis also undercuts the importance of children's making an effort and working hard in school.

Consider Benjamin Bloom's conclusion after forty years of researching school learning in the United States and abroad. He writes in *Developing Talent in Young People* that 95 percent of all students can learn equally well if they have a positive environment for learning.[10]

Ninety-five percent! Why, that includes almost all students! That's right. And this conclusion comes from a man whose research and recommendations led to the highly regarded Head Start program, a man so eminent in education that he has been called "the foremost educational researcher after Piaget."[11]

The only students Bloom excludes from his 95 percent are the 1 to 2 percent whose exceptional gifts allow them to learn very rapidly and the 2 to 3 percent whose severe physical or emotional handicaps keep them from learning. Bloom writes, "The middle 95% of school students become very similar in terms of their measured achievement, learning ability, rate of learning, and motivation for further learning when provided with *favorable learning conditions.*"[12]

What does this mean? For parents, it should provide a lot of reassurance because, at the very least, it means that our children have the ability to do well in school. Jaime Escalante understood this very well about his own students. He related that he found most "gifted" students to be no different from "average" students, "except in their ability to score high on tracking tests."

Escalante had so little concern over what we call "ability" that he didn't even review the standardized test scores of students coming into his program. Nor did he select students from the "gifted" or "high IQ track." Escalante ignored these criteria because he believed "that tracking is unworkable and unproven as a guarantee that students will be channeled into a program best suited for them." Instead, he picked students for his program by their *ganas*, or desire to succeed and to learn, and then he expected them to work hard.[13]

An inspiring story appeared in the *Washington Post* about a successful young man whose mother had instilled in him a desire and willingness to work hard.[14]

Stephen F. Smith went from the "depths of welfare" in Washington, D.C., to a scholarship at Dartmouth College and on to the University of Virginia Law School, where he graduated in the top ten of his class. This twenty-four-year-old black Supreme Court clerk attributed his climb out of the welfare cycle to his mother's "no-excuses approach."

Plagued by asthma as a child, Smith was frequently in and out of the hospital. He tells about returning home from one such hospital stay during third grade. He didn't feel like studying for an oral math quiz he was to have the next day on the multiplication tables, but his mother insisted that he take the quiz with the rest of the class. She told him that he was not going to sleep until he knew the multiplication tables for the quiz.

They stayed up together until he knew them all, even though it took until 4:30 A.M. The next day, even though Stephen raised his hand to answer many of the questions, the teacher never called on him. But what he remembered best from that day were his mother's words of praise when she heard what had happened. "You knew the answers," she told him. "You didn't need any special treatment."

One of the most important things parents can do is instill in their children the willingness and capacity for hard work. This hard work ethic is the gift Stephen Smith's mother gave him. It took him through school, college, and law school. It propelled him to a Supreme Court clerkship.

All of us can instill that same work ethic in our children, if we understand how important it is. We can help them develop values, attitudes, and habits that will take them through school and stay with them as adults. Children can learn that applying themselves in school is their work, their job. They can acquire positive feelings about doing their work and going to school prepared. And through this approach to school, children can develop the capacity for hard work and perseverance, sticking with a job until it's done.

The point is that parents can give children a work ethic that will help them in school and later, one that will serve them for life. They probably won't even know where it came from. And they don't need to.

In the introduction, we told about Ray and Eleanor Dunn, two teachers who helped their son Kevin develop strong work habits and study strategies so he could do well in school. After reading the introduction with Kevin, Eleanor wrote to us: "I don't think he's thought much about where his work ethic and motivation come from. He has to take most of the credit, of course, but for the first time I think he started to consider that maybe his parents had a little to do with his success, too!"

Chapter 6
Believing in Your Child

What expectations do you have for your child? What are the present and future pictures of your child in your mind? Look carefully; these pictures are self-fulfilling prophecies – children absorb them and conform to them.

–Faith Clark and Cecil Clark
Hassle-Free Homework

Children respond to the expectations we hold for them.
–Secretary of Education Richard Riley
Address at Georgetown University, 1994

As we saw in Chapter 2, belief and expectation are at the heart of parents teaching their children to walk and talk. Parents know that their children will succeed. That knowledge frees the parent to encourage efforts and frees the child to make efforts unclouded by fear of failure. Positive beliefs and expectations are just as necessary in helping a child learn to work hard and achieve in school.

We don't usually think of expectations and beliefs as things we *do* or can do. Rather, we think of them as being beyond our control – things that *are* – not actions. Truthfully, one of the most important things parents can do is to hold – or choose to hold – positive expectations and beliefs about their children, because expectation and belief powerfully shape performance.

The Power of Expectation

Pygmalion in the Classroom is a classic on the power of expectation in learning. Two episodes from the book bear recounting here.

The first is a story from the government workplace illustrating the effect that belief and expectation can have on performance.[1] Back in 1890, the Hollerith tabulating machine was installed at the U.S. Census Bureau. Hollerith, the inventor of this typewriter-like machine, believed that learning to use the new machine would be taxing and difficult. He let the clerks in the Census Bureau know his belief and told them that after training, he expected them to be able to punch only about 550 cards in a day.

Following their two weeks of training, the workers proved him right. They were able to punch just that many cards, 550 a day, with relative ease. Five weeks later they could produce more, about 700 cards, but only "at great emotional cost."

Soon, however, the Census Bureau expanded the department and brought in 200 more workers to learn to use the Hollerith machine. After receiving only three days of training, the new clerks were easily producing, without tension, 2,100 cards – nearly four times the capacity of the original trainees! The reason for their great production? No one had told them of the imaginary 550-card limit. Unlike the other workers, they had no strong negative expectations to limit their production.

The main story in *Pygmalion in the Classroom* is perhaps the best known, if somewhat controversial, study of teacher expectation as self-fulfilling prophecy.[2] Robert Rosenthal and Leonore Jacobson gave more than 500 students in Oak School, a public elementary school in a lower-income community, a standard but little known IQ test, Flanagan's Tests of General Ability. Then they randomly chose 20 percent of the students and gave them falsely high test scores. All teachers of grades one to six were told that those students were expected to soon "spurt ahead" in their learning.

Planting this seed of expectation produced positive results, but the most startling were for the younger students. Rosenthal and Jacobson found that at the time of retesting a year later, 47 percent of the first and second graders on their list had gained 20 or more IQ points, whereas only 19 percent of their classmates had made such a jump.

A large number of the students on the list continued to improve in performance the following year, according to retesting at the end of the second year. Interestingly, among the students who benefited the most from those changes in teacher beliefs were those who were or appeared to be Mexican, the only minority group represented at this school.

The researchers attributed the changes to teacher expectation – a change in the way the teachers saw those students. "Nothing was done directly for the disadvantaged child at Oak School. There was no crash program to improve his reading ability, no special lesson plan, no extra time for tutoring, no trips to museums or art galleries. There was only the belief that the children bore watching, that they had intellectual competencies that would, in due course, be revealed."[3]

The Power of Teacher Expectations

The best teachers seem to understand, either consciously or intuitively, the importance of believing in their students. Jaime Escalante is once again a good example of this. In an article on his program, Escalante commented that the movie *Stand and Deliver* showed that disadvantaged students can work hard and achieve academic excellence if we expect them to. He wrote that it laid to rest the unhelpful myth that expecting academic excellence from poverty-level students puts too great a strain on their "fragile" self-esteem. "When students of any race, ethnicity, or economic status are expected to work hard, they usually rise to the occasion, devote themselves to the task, and do the work. If we expect kids to be losers, they will be losers; if we expect them to be winners, they will be winners."[4]

Similarly, Bonnie Bracey, a Virginia teacher, tells about teaching a gifted and talented class in which some students didn't actually fall into this category on the basis of their test scores. "I made no distinction between those who were identified as gifted and talented and those who weren't. . . . I told the class, 'Everyone has different talents and abilities. I don't know what all of yours are, but we're all going to work hard to discover them.'"[5] The results? The children who progressed the most in their achievement that year were the very ones who weren't identified as gifted and talented.

When schools take this approach, they also get results. Look at what's happening in six "Paideia" schools in Chattanooga, Tennessee. These schools don't divide kids according to test scores and "ability" groupings. This is a principle of the Paideia school approach started by the psychologist Mortimer Adler over ten years ago. Instead of grouping students, these schools give all students the same curriculum at the same level – no "dumbed down" classes for the "slow" learners. Expectations are high for all. William Raspberry wrote about this, "The children are expected to achieve honor-student results, and they do."[6]

Georgia Tech University has tried something similar in its summer "bridge" program for minority engineering students.[7] The university used to scale back the work in this program to allow for the students' special needs and problems. Now the program treats the students as bright and capable. The results have been so successful that nonminority engineering students are now asking that everyone be allowed to take the program.

If these programs make such a difference because of teacher and school expectations, think how much more powerful parents' expectations are.

The Power of Parent Beliefs

A friend of ours shared a moving story with us about how she and her husband continued to believe in their son, even though he appeared to have serious problems. She wrote:

"As you know, Matthew did not produce words until he was three years old. Nor did we know for certain if he understood words because he appeared to be shut off from language in general. But I read to him anyway. When his language emerged, it was in whole sentences.

"When he was in second grade, because his speech was still impaired, he was placed in a very low reading group (rhyming words only, no sentences – the red bedspread, the loose goose, etc.). I was upset at this placement because, after all, his comprehension was not impaired, only his pronunciation. Why should school stunt his reading development by placing him in such a low reading group?

"He surprised me one day by reading aloud from a library book about snakes. The sentences were complex. I told his teachers, who did not believe me and did not release him from his rhyming treadmill. They said he couldn't read.

"So I decided to bypass the school reading experience and supplement entirely at home. I got some interesting books at about fifth-grade reading level, and he and I took turns reading aloud. Within three months, he read his first book all alone. It was *Count Dracula*. It remains his favorite book.

"He went on from that to *Frankenstein* and *Robinson Crusoe*. The language patterns were already there from all the reading he had heard, but at the rate he was going in school he might have become a nonreader."

Matthew was lucky. He had a mother who believed in him completely and knew how to help him rise above the expectations his teachers held for him and realize his capabilities. Through his mother's belief in him, he began to find success in reading and eventually in school.

Silent Messages

When we see how powerful beliefs and expectations are, we – both parents and teachers – naturally want to hold positive beliefs about our children. But what happens when we don't believe in a child or student? What happens when we *say* we do, but we know there's little conviction behind our words? No matter what we say, in a very deep way, our children know what we feel about them.

Albert Mehrabian, a professor and researcher now at UCLA, contends that 93 percent of our communication of liking and not liking is not in the words we speak but in our tone of voice, facial expression, and body language. In his book *Silent Messages*, Mehrabian writes: "only 7% of our communication is what we 'say,' the actual words, while 38% is tonal and 55% totally non-verbal."[8] If Mehrabian's percentages are even close, they give us a lot to think about.

One of the most common problems for children trying to improve their schoolwork is overcoming their parents' negative judgments, disappointment, and negative expectations for them. Some parents openly show their anger and disappointment. For instance, one father spoke openly and harshly in front of his son about how badly the boy had done the previous year and how angry he, the father, was. Other parents show their feelings more subtly, but we should be assured that if we have those feelings, they will be communicated.

In *The Seven Habits of Highly Effective People*, Stephen Covey tells about a time he and his wife failed to believe in one of their sons.[9]

Covey writes that the boy was doing poorly in all areas of his life – in academics, in his social life, in sports. Covey and his wife Sandra tried encouraging him and they tried advising him, but nothing seemed to help. Finally, they saw the basic problem: that no matter what they said to their son to encourage him, deep down they believed that something was wrong with him, that he wasn't bright and capable. Their son was experiencing the power of the unspoken or silent messages his parents were sending him.

When the parents realized how they felt, they knew that they had to change themselves – their own feelings – if they were to help him. Using deep thought and prayer, Covey says that they began to let go and trust that their son would develop in his own time and way. Then they started to see him as the capable person he was. Covey relates that slowly, over several years, their son began to change. He grew in confidence and, over time, excelled in all areas of his life, becoming an outstanding student, leader, and athlete.

It's hard to imagine a better example to demonstrate the great power that parents' beliefs and expectations can have on their children. Covey and his wife began to change only after seeing that their silent messages to their son were strongly negative. They understood the connection between those messages and their beliefs and were able to change their beliefs.

Two Powerful Tools for Changing Beliefs

But how do you change your feelings? How do you change your expectations? The Coveys used deep thought and prayer to change their beliefs and feelings about their son. So those are obvious possibilities. We have found two other powerful tools for this – *visualization*, what we imagine, and *self-talk*, what we say to ourselves. It's natural to use the imagination to hold an image of a child, and it's natural to say things about your child. These are two faculties or functions of the mind that we all use regularly, and this is how they work.

Visualization is based on past experience. Parents see their children in a particular way in their imaginations. They carry this image of their children in their minds. They "feel" and believe that the children are either competent or incompetent, strong or weak, intelligent or unintelligent, dependable or unreliable.

Self-talk is also based on past experience and how parents view their children. Parents say things to themselves like: "Mary's never on time." "Jim is terrible at math." "He always does his work at the last minute." "She just wants to watch TV. That's all she ever does." "He never does his homework unless I make him."

It's natural to do these things – to use visualization and self-talk. The problems arise when we engage in these two activities unconsciously and negatively. We don't decide to hold a negative image of our children, and we don't decide to say negative things. In fact, we don't even realize that we are doing these things. But because it's so easy to see the flaws of people we're around a lot, we find ourselves focusing on our children's shortcomings, seeing what's wrong with them rather than recognizing and emphasizing their strengths.

At the start of this chapter we said that one of the most important things parents can do in working with children is to hold – or choose to hold – positive expectations and beliefs. The reason for this is simple. If you don't decide to hold positive beliefs, you will almost certainly hold negative ones.

So here is the choice you can make: you can unconsciously hold negative beliefs and expectations, or you can choose to hold positive beliefs about your child. You can use these same faculties or activities of the mind positively and consciously. You can make a calculated choice to say and imagine positive, helpful things about your children. And you can do these things again and again until your beliefs and expectations change.

A good first step to change the habits of seeing weaknesses and saying negative things about a child is to focus on and list the child's strengths, best qualities, and positive habits (use the form on page 62). What qualities does your child show in different situations? Is he a loyal friend? A team player? Does she have independence and personal integrity? Does your son show responsibility in doing his chores? Does your daughter show compassion for others? What qualities do you admire in your child?

Just doing this exercise is helpful in changing feelings and beliefs about children. The list you've come up with can also serve as affirmations for self-talk and as a guide to concrete and effective visualizations.

Self-Talk

Here's how you use the list of strengths for self-talk:

If your list looks like this:
John is a loyal friend.
He is considerate of others.
He cheerfully helps clean the house.
He helps his sister with her homework.

Your affirmations might look like this:
I like John.
I appreciate his strengths.
I value his friendship.
I can see that he has a number of wonderful qualities.
I like the way he's loyal to his friends.
I appreciate his considerate nature.
I enjoy the way he helps his sister.
I appreciate the way he cheerfully cleans up.
I enjoy watching John grow and develop his strengths and
    good qualities.
I love my son.
He is wonderful.

When constructing affirmations, be sure to:

- state the self-talk phrases positively

- put them in the present tense

- own the feelings they express

For them to be effective, you'll want to repeat them many times, so write them down as a reminder. Carry them around in your

The strengths, virtues, and qualities I see and admire in my child include:

_____

_____

_____

_____

_____

_____

_____

_____

_____

_____

_____

_____

_____

pocket. Post them in places where you'll see them. Read them. Say them to yourself. Repeat them aloud. Repeat them silently.

And when you say the affirmations, say them with feeling, as if you really mean them. Remember that these statements are replacing the unconscious, negative things we parents usually say about our children. Say them with as much feeling and conviction as you can.

Visualization (or Positive Use of the Imagination)

Psychologists tell us that a vividly imagined experience is no different in most ways, to the mind and the nervous system, from a real one.[10] This suggests that if you vividly imagine admiring and appreciating someone you actually hold a negative image of, your feelings will slowly begin to change. If this is true, you can begin to change the image you hold of your child through visualization.

You can, through your imagination, choose to hold different expectations and beliefs. Change the feelings, expectations, and beliefs, and eventually you'll change the silent message you deliver. To do this:

- Go over the list of your child's admirable qualities.

- Get them clearly in mind.

- Imagine that your child is standing in front of you.

- Generate strong feelings of affection and admiration toward your child.

- Enjoy, appreciate, and celebrate each of those habits and qualities.

Remember, you do these things to change yourself, your feelings, and your beliefs, not to change your child. When you use the imagination, when you use self-talk, you are working to recognize your child's strengths and good qualities, to appreciate and affirm them. If you see and appreciate those qualities and strengths, the child will also be likely to see, appreciate, and further develop those parts of him- or herself.

You want strong, positive affection, expectation, and belief to underlie all your work, all your involvement with your child. It's at the heart of a strong positive parent-child relationship (or any relationship, for that matter.)

Either or both of these approaches might be used. But simply understanding the importance of expectation and *wanting* to change goes a long way toward finding what will work.

Psycho-Cybernetics by Maxwell Maltz and *What to Say When You Talk to Yourself* by Shad Helmstetter are a couple of good resources for more information on visualization and self-talk.[11] Strategy C of this book shows how to use these two techniques to help youngsters change the way they feel about school subjects they dislike and performance situations they feel nervous about.

Major Points to Remember

- Expectations, feelings, and beliefs exert a powerful influence on performance.

- They are communicated powerfully on a nonverbal level.

- Change your expectations, feelings, and beliefs and you automatically change the message you give.

- You can change through positive, conscious use of the imagination and self-talk.

Part III
Encouraging Efforts

- Habit: The Key to Motivation

- Establishing the Homework Habit

Chapter 7
Habit: The Key to Motivation

The great thing then in all education, is to make our nervous system our ally instead of our enemy. . . . For this we must make automatic and habitual, as early as possible, as many useful actions as we can, *and guard against the growing into ways that are likely to be disadvantageous to us.*

–William James
Writings 1878–1899

The Problem

Adrienne came to the Achievement Center the summer after her son Andrew had had an "absolutely horrible" fifth-grade year. His report card that year looked as if it "belonged to a different child": he had made a low grade in math and in another subject. More important, Andrew had grown both to dislike math and to doubt his math ability. Adrienne was concerned about his poor performance, especially in math, so she enrolled the boy in a summer math class.

The real problem showed up on the second day of class when Andrew came without his homework assignment. The boy admitted that he hadn't done the work. He said that he didn't feel like doing it.

The same thing happened again the next day. When asked, "Is this what happens in school?" Andrew was honest. "Yeah, I guess it is. If I like the work, I do it. But if I don't like it, I don't." He went on to say that he usually found math homework boring.

Andrew admitted that there was a part of him that wanted to do schoolwork. This part of him would tug gently at his shirt-sleeve, so to speak, and say, "You better do your work." He said that he didn't like going to school without having finished his homework. But, at the same time, there was another part of him, a much bigger part, pulling and saying, "I don't want to do that stuff. I'd rather watch TV. I'd rather play ball. I'd rather play Nintendo or read. I'd rather do anything than school-work."

This is the problem most children have with schoolwork. And Andrew wasn't yet in sixth grade. What happens when students grow older and haven't learned to work? Is it different for them?

A few years ago, the *Washington Post* ran the following head-line: "Even at a Top School, the Temptation Is Just to Slide By." It was the first of a series of articles on Bethesda–Chevy Chase High School, a public school in an affluent Maryland suburb of Washington, D.C.[1] At this school, 46 percent of the 1,000 stu-dents polled said that they saw themselves as "sliding by," not working to their full potential, content with low B's and C's in their classes.

A senior gave these reasons for his mediocre achievement, and they probably sound familiar: "Lack of motivation. I don't like to work. It takes too much time." Many students claimed that they felt "no urgency from outside or within" themselves to achieve in school. Like Andrew, the older students justified making other activities more important than doing schoolwork – things like social life, after-school jobs, sports.

The problem is no different for students from less affluent backgrounds. A 1992 editorial quoted Sue Berryman, a profes-sor at Columbia Teachers College, on why many at-risk chil-dren from low-income families fail:

It's not that they lack the intellectual capacity to succeed in school, she said, but that "they do not *want* to be – or do not see the *point* in being – good" in the subjects we prescribe for them.

Her belief is that these children perceive no link between classroom exertion and their own future.[2]

Someone has to lead children to want to do their work. That means making the daily tug to do schoolwork stronger than the pull to just enjoy themselves. Youngsters will understand and accept the need to work hard only if someone important to them is convinced of the value of schoolwork, communicates that value to them, and leads them to the habit of working. Parents do this best.

We parents may feel uncomfortable making our priorities our children's priorities. But sometimes that's our job – to make decisions for children about what's most important in the long run for them to lead successful, happy lives. We need to realize that it's our job, our role, to make important decisions for children, to communicate those decisions, and sometimes to impose them on the children for their good. An English teacher at Bethesda–Chevy Chase High School put it this way: "If parents don't follow through at home . . . I don't think there is anything the educational community can do to energize someone to work."[3]

And parents don't have be well educated themselves to do this. A middle school principal in Florida writes:

> Parents have to tell children on a daily basis and emphasize to them the value of an education. I use my father as an example. My father could not read or write. Yet three of his four children graduated from college. . . . His point to me throughout my younger life was "you are going to get an education, an education is important to you and it's important to you for the following reasons."[4]

This father was firmly convinced that an education was important to his children, so he could communicate those reasons effectively.

The Solution — Homework as a Habit, Not a Decision

A common way to try to motivate children to do schoolwork is through rewards and punishments. We offer rewards for good performance: "I'll give you a Nintendo game, a new outfit, a bicycle [even a car] if you make the honor roll." We threaten them with loss of privileges or grounding if grades are poor: "Your grades are terrible. You're grounded!"

But then we turn the task of doing daily schoolwork over to them. We assume that they're going to make the right choice on a daily basis – the choice to do their schoolwork. When we do this, we're not really involved (except to punish them for poor results) because we don't make sure that they do their work. In fact, we usually don't know whether a child is actually doing the work or not until we get a progress report or a report card.

It's important to understand that the problems come from allowing children to make the decision every day: will I work or will I do something else – something I'd rather do. It's a mistake. It's the big mistake most of us make. By not monitoring children's work on a daily basis and by not helping them get this work done, we allow them to choose to do their work or not. Because most children aren't capable of making this decision rationally, they make their choices based on what they feel like doing.

Allowing children to repeatedly make the wrong choice weakens their will to work. Philosopher William James wrote that he knew of no more unhappy person than the one who has to make decisions about whether to do the simple, basic things of life. These things, James wrote, should be "turned over to habit."[5]

That's exactly what we want our children to do – turn their daily work into habit by doing it repeatedly. And by doing their work repeatedly, students will not only develop the habit of working, they will also become good at it. Their performance will improve. Aristotle wrote: "We are what we repeatedly do. Excellence is not an act but a habit."[6]

The parents' task is to lead children to doing daily schoolwork so that working becomes a habit, not a choice. It's that simple. We want children to complete their homework every day until they don't have to think about it – like brushing their teeth. To do that effectively, we have to be clear that this habit is our real goal. This is the essence of the parents' role in motivating children to work hard in school.

The problem that Andrew and the students at Bethesda–Chevy Chase High School had was that work never got to be a habit for them. It remained one of the many things vying for their time and attention. Luckily for Andrew, his mother changed that for him.

Adrienne came to see that what Andrew needed was to be led to the point where work wasn't a decision but a daily habit, where doing his work was automatic and required much less conscious thought. She also realized that she was the key to this. In fact, she said that she was going to be ruthless in making sure that Andrew did his work, while giving him the support and attention he needed to succeed.

That fall, Adrienne regularly explained to Andrew that his schoolwork was his job and that even though he might not feel like doing his homework, he must. She told him that he was forming habits that would serve him for the rest of his life. She also made it clear that she would help him.

In the beginning, it wasn't easy. Adrienne said that she had to fight and hassle with her son over homework every day for a good while. But she was convinced that this was his job and that he had to do it.

About a month into his sixth-grade year, things got a little easier. Andrew got used to the fact that he had to do the work. He was lucky that year, for he had a teacher who expected a lot, emphasized that students must do all their work faithfully, and communicated regularly with parents. Because of this and because he knew that his mother was serious about his doing all his assignments, he did them. That fall, his mother reported that 99 percent of the time, all assignments were done. Luckily, she knew that she could count on the teacher to let her know about any missing work.

Everything went well until about January or February, when Andrew became less willing to do homework. Adrienne had to pressure him more and more frequently until finally they reached an impasse over a book report assignment. When the boy announced that he just wasn't going to do the report, she blew up. "I have two other kids to take care of as well," she told him. "I want you to grow up to hold down a responsible, good-paying job, but I can't do the work for you. You're on your own!" She walked out of the room.

About ten minutes after the explosion, Andrew came into her room, put his arms around her, and said, "Mom, I'm sorry. I'm gonna try harder."

The book report was written, and for the rest of the year, Andrew completed all his homework. Of course, there were still struggles from time to time. But slowly, working became a habit.

Adrienne could see real changes in her son. Some days he would even come home and announce, "I've got something I need to do this afternoon, so I want to get my homework out of the way first."

She would then congratulate him on having such a great attitude: "I'm proud of you."

At other times, the boy would say, "I really don't want to do this work."

"Andrew, this is what is required of you," his mother would tell him. "This is your job and you must do it." Then she would recite the litany of positive effects he would gain from doing his homework. Even though she tired of reciting the litany, and he tired of hearing it, he knew that, like it or not, he had to do his work.

In the last quarter of the school year, Andrew made the honor roll, along with his younger brother Eric. For Andrew, it was the first time.

Adrienne said that when the two boys brought their honor roll certificates home, she felt proud of them. She added, "But you know, I was also proud of myself. I felt we had accomplished something. I was part of it."

What did this mother do to bring her child to this level of success?

- She understood that habit was the goal – the habit of doing each day's work thoroughly and well.

- She accepted that it was her unique role to lead him to this habit.

- By focusing on habit as her goal, she could ignore the immediate results – grades.

- She allowed no excuses. She was ruthless and at the same time positive in her involvement because her attention was on work, not on grades.

- Because she was convinced of her role, she was convincing.

The next year, Adrienne found that she had to continue her involvement. She learned that habits don't come easily, and involvement is not short term. One good year, especially for a sixth or seventh grader, may not be enough. If you're serious about your involvement, it's important to realize that you may be looking at two to three years of work.

Making Schoolwork the Top Priority

To make homework a priority for children, parents can help by limiting the number of concerns they raise. You don't want homework buried among a long list of mildly important issues

– things such as children cleaning their rooms, washing dishes, doing laundry, fixing meals, cleaning the house, or washing the car. If you find yourself raising most, many, or even several of these concerns, remember that although schoolwork is more important than any of them, that may not be clear to children.

When our daughter entered the ninth grade in a demanding school, she also began to run on the cross-country team and started flute lessons. Although we wanted schoolwork first in her priorities, we also wanted her to be able to explore her other interests. It was easy to see that daily homework plus almost two hours of running, an hour of flute practice, and household chores added up to trouble.

It was obvious where her priorities were. Homework and household chores were at the bottom of her list. She enjoyed her flute lessons and practice. But running was her strongest interest at that time.

We wanted to make homework and schoolwork come first, but to make that stick, there needed to be as few real issues as possible. To avoid a situation where homework was just one issue along with doing the dishes and raking the yard, we did something that may seem drastic. We relieved her of all household chores except cleaning her room and making her lunches. We made it clear why she had no chores. And we were clear about why we did it – to limit issues. She resumed chores in the summers and gradually has taken on more duties at home, but in the beginning, this was a great help in keeping our focus and in keeping her focused on schoolwork.

Obviously, many kids won't have such busy schedules and will have time to help out around the house. It's reasonable to expect them to. But it's also important to keep your priorities straight, to know what you consider important. Are household chores as important as getting an education? Obviously not. But it's easy to give them as much importance in a child's mind if we're always nagging the child to do a number of different things.

A study of Asian children who came to America and performed well in some of our inner-city schools found that the parents played a key role in their children's success. Despite the parents' "lack of education" and inability to help with the content of the homework, they "set standards and facilitate their children's studies by assuming responsibility for chores and other practical considerations."[7] In this way, these parents ensured that their children did the work that was more important — schoolwork.

As children grow older, more and more activities compete with homework for first priority, so making the choice to do schoolwork is even harder for them. You'll find that drawing lines when necessary is part of showing children that you care about their schoolwork and about them. It's part of helping them develop the habit of doing their schoolwork. If you are convinced of your role and hold youngsters to their work, they will follow your lead.

Remember, research shows that children want their parents to help them direct their lives well. If you don't do this, it's unlikely that children will make schoolwork a priority — because most young people don't naturally put their schoolwork first.

In addition to limiting the use of television, which is covered in the next chapter, there are at least three areas where parents play this role of drawing lines — extracurricular activities, dating or social life, and after-school jobs.

Competing with Extracurricular Activities

Drawing lines for children often means putting sports, music, acting, and other activities in perspective and in line, firmly behind schoolwork in importance.

During her sophomore year, our daughter missed school one Friday for the county indoor track meet and still had lots of work to make up when Monday night rolled around. Late Monday night she sat exhausted, putting the final touches on a Shakespeare oral presentation for the next day, with work in other subjects still untouched. It was then that we realized that she could, and should, have missed her track practice that day to finish her work.

The next day, when all the pressure was off, we talked about this, explaining that we would sometimes have to draw lines when other things vied for top priority with her schoolwork. "We really support you in your running, but sometimes you might have to miss a practice – or even a meet – if it interferes too much with your schoolwork."

"OK," she said, "but that's your priority, it's not mine."

Interestingly, she later showed that she had, in some way at least, accepted "our priority." The next week, right before the state indoor track meet, she chose to miss a track practice because she had too much schoolwork that night. A few days later we happened to see a birthday note she had written to her grandfather, saying, "I love the long-distance runs we're doing in track now. But I had to miss one last week because I had too much homework."

Competing with Social Life

For one mother, the issue with her high school junior was dating. She and her daughter had an ongoing battle about Stacie's wanting to date during the week. Her mother forbade it and also limited phone conversations. Stacie argued, "But my grades are good! I'm making A's and B's. So why can't I go out during the week?"

"That's exactly why your grades are good," her mother replied. "Because you stay focused on your schoolwork during the week."

Stacie's mother reported that halfway through that school year her daughter stopped making an issue of dating in the school week.

Competing with After-School Jobs

Another major competitor for students' time is after-school jobs. According to a 1992 *Newsweek* cover story, "Teens are twice as likely to work as they were in 1950."[8] Almost two-thirds of the high school seniors surveyed worked five or more hours a week during the school year. Surprisingly, youngsters were not taking those jobs out of basic needs: only 10 percent of those surveyed said that they were using this money for college. Another 6 percent said that they were helping with family living expenses, but most worked simply to have more spending money.

For most students, doing this work meant sacrificing their studies. One student summed up what many seemed to feel: "School's important, but so's money. Homework doesn't pay." Though the jobs did "pay," they also had a cost. The writers reported that more than five hours of work correlated with lower school achievement for most students.

In a *Washington Post* editorial, Robert J. Samuelson commented, "Most students cannot do well at both school and demanding jobs. . . . After-school jobs mean students study less: They don't cultivate the skills increasingly required for good-paying jobs."[9]

Samuelson also told a story from David McCullough's biography of Harry Truman. When he was fourteen years old, Truman took a job at a local drug store. After three months, John Truman, his father, stepped in and told him that "he had done enough. Better that he concentrate on his studies."

Truman's father understood the importance of an education, of not sacrificing a long-term good for a short-term reward. As Samuelson writes at the end of his editorial, "John Truman had it right." He not only understood how important studies are, he also helped his son back on track, directing him to put his attention where it belonged – on schoolwork.

Chapter 8
Establishing the Homework Habit

*Nowhere is the family's commitment to accomplishment and educa-
tion more evident than in time spent on homework.*
–Nathan Caplan, Marcella H. Choy, and John K. Whitmore
"Indochinese Refugee Families and Academic Achievement"

There are a number of things parents can do, and will want
to do, to lead their children to the habit of doing their
work thoroughly and well.

Give Efforts Your Positive Attention

The chief way parents encourage hard work is by giving their
positive and undivided attention to what children are learning,
to the efforts children are making. This is true when the
children are learning to walk and talk, and it is also true when
they are doing schoolwork, but there is a difference. With
infants, giving attention is natural and parents aren't likely to
regard it as a sacrifice. As children grow older, however, parents have to make more conscious choices. It's harder to give
positive attention, and involvement seems much more of a bur-
den or sacrifice.

Diane said that she and her husband George had always
emphasized to their children the importance of doing their

homework. They bought desks for their fifth-grade son R. J. and their seventh-grade daughter Tara. They put the desks in their rooms so the children would have a quiet place to study.

The family's routine after dinner was a familiar one. The children went to their rooms to finish any homework they hadn't done in the afternoon while the parents finished up chores and then relaxed in front of the TV. One by one, as they finished their work, the children joined their parents at the television. Although they often tried to check their children's homework, they were usually told: "It's OK. I don't need any help."

Despite their efforts, Diane said that she felt vaguely out of touch with her children and their lives. Still, she thought that everything was going OK with school – until the third quarter of Tara's seventh-grade year, when they got a wake-up call in the form of a report card. That quarter, Tara's grades had all fallen – to C's, D,'s, and F's. Her parents were stunned.

They learned from Tara and her teachers that she had been hanging out with a group of kids who didn't think that homework was important, and she had not been focusing on her schoolwork at all for several months. Although they talked repeatedly with their daughter and tried many things to help her improve her grades, nothing worked.

During the summer before her eighth-grade year, they enrolled Tara in a math program to improve her math skills. That fall, Diane told us what had happened to Tara in the seventh grade and said, "I'd like to do something to get back in touch with her."

Jack suggested, "One thing you could do is have your children do their homework in a central location with you and your husband nearby and available to help rather than sending them off to work alone in their rooms."

Diane said, "But we thought they needed the quiet of an isolated setting to do their best work."

Then we discussed the advantages of getting the children out of their rooms and into a central location to study. Doing this:

- shows both symbolically and in reality that homework is important

- allows parents to be involved and in touch with the child's work

- gives children the sense that they are not alone in their efforts

- encourages the family to turn off the TV

Diane could see these benefits and decided to talk it over with her husband. They knew that this kind of change wouldn't be easy. It would mean adjusting their evening routine, making what, at the time, seemed like sacrifices. But they agreed that it was worth a try.

Diane and George then announced to the children that they were going to make homework the evening event! Instead of watching television or playing a game, homework would be the family event on school nights. The children would be limited to watching two TV shows a week.

The first night after dinner, they cleared the kitchen table, and both of the children sat down with their homework. Diane sat down at the table as well with something to read. Not long after, George joined them. Soon Kyle, the youngest, wanted to join them to do his fifteen minutes worth of kindergarten work.

After a week or so of doing their work at the kitchen table, the children started asking their parents to quiz them on material they were being tested on. They even took some interest in each other's schoolwork. For example, Tara would sometimes quiz R. J. on his vocabulary work for the day.

Weeks passed. The children did not rebel about doing their work at the table. They had grown used to the routine and sometimes even seemed eager to sit down together. The parents reported that their children started to talk spontaneously about things that had happened at school in ways that they never had when Diane had simply asked them, "How was your day?"

The parents also went from simply being present while the children worked to helping them. One night Diane would help Tara with a social studies report while her husband went over a reading assignment with R. J. When Kyle finished his work, they found other things for him to do at the table – drawing or coloring.

Diane reported that the family members became more involved in one another's lives. No one seemed to miss flopping in front of the TV. The children watched two shows during the week, if they remembered, and they didn't ask to have the television on at other times.

Progress report time came, and all of Tara's grades were up – even though she had transferred into the school's challenging talented and gifted (TAG) classes.

Adjustments have come up from time to time. For example, when R. J. had a soccer game, his dad would go with him and Diane would stay home to work with Tara and Kyle. But basically the whole family spent most of their weeknights sitting down to do homework together.

Diane said that she and her husband noticed the change for them. "We really felt in touch with our children's lives. We learned about their days at school. Homework was no longer a struggle – the children didn't have the feeling they had to go it alone, so homework became easier. I think the children really felt we were all in this together. They felt their work was important to us and that they didn't have to do it all alone."

The changes this family made were simple ones:

- The children shifted to a central place in the house to do their homework.

- The family rearranged its schedule so homework could be done in the evening when the parents were home rather than right after school.

• Homework became the evening event. The parents made themselves available, both by sitting with the children as they worked and by showing interest, by giving their attention.

• The TV was turned off for everyone.

Pick a Central Place

Location! location! location! They say it's important in real estate. It's equally or more important in homework. Why? Having children do their work in a central location shows that it's important. It "tells" them in a powerful way that parents value the work they have to do enough to put it central in the house and make it central to the evening.

One of the most common errors parents make is to send their children off to their rooms to do homework. When they do this, they give a powerful negative message about homework, especially if they sit and watch TV while their children work. The message is: "We'll have a good time here in front of the TV while you go and do your work." It's small wonder that children come to view homework as punishment. Why, they could be watching television if they didn't have to do "that work." And although parents might tell children that their schoolwork is important, they show children what they truly value by where they put their attention.

The other problems with sending children away to work are that it's hard to monitor their work and it's hard to be involved or help in any way.

One parent at a private school where Marsha was teaching was shocked when her sixth-grade son came home with an F in reading. She told the guidance counselor, "I don't know what's going on. He goes to his room every night and spends two hours doing his homework." Yet he was failing in-class quizzes on the novel the class was reading because he hadn't read the assigned chapters. When the mother checked on what her son was doing, she found out that he was listening to tapes in his room and doing only the homework that came easily.

Location is extremely important for a parent who is serious about being involved in schoolwork. Being present in a central location and being willing to help is a good beginning.

Do Homework When Parents Are Home

When parents get home they are tired and often don't want to deal with homework. It's common for parents to want children to finish their schoolwork in the afternoon. That's what Diane used to have the children do. They'd come home from school, have a short break, and then do their homework. Then with all the work out of the way, everyone could relax and watch TV.

Diane said that she and George came to see that if they were going to be involved in their children's homework, the bulk of the work would have to be done after dinner, not before. This arrangement worked out better for the children as well as for the work. As she put it, "The last thing anyone wants to do when they come home from work is do work. Children are no different. My kids love having a break now in the afternoon to play, be with their friends. Then they're ready to settle down with us to do their homework. And it becomes something special because we're all involved in it."

For most of us, this is a hard decision to make, for it often means changing our entire evening routine. One mother at a parent involvement workshop said bluntly, "Just how long are you supposed to do this? I don't like the idea of changing my evenings this way. I come home tired, and I want to relax."

This may seem like quite a sacrifice in the beginning. But if you're serious about helping your child, you'll want to try it.

Make Homework the Evening Event

In 1988, a study was made of the children of Indochinese refugees who settled in five urban areas in the United States during the 1980s.[1] These children came to the United States not knowing the language or the culture. They entered the inner-city schools and in two to three years were dramatically successful.

Researchers determined their success by looking at their grade point averages and their test scores. They had impressive overall grade point averages – 3.2 as a group, on a 4.0 scale. And after only a few years of speaking English, they scored in the top 50 percent of students taking the California Achievement Test – in all subjects.

Their secret? According to the researchers, these children had parents who valued their schoolwork and gave it a lot of attention.

Although the parents couldn't help much with the actual homework – most spoke little English – they could help their children set goals for their studies and follow through to reach those goals. They did simple, practical things like seeing that the table was cleared after dinner and homework begun. The parents made homework the first priority in the home. They made sure that it dominated household activities on weeknights. The researchers wrote: "Nowhere is the family's commitment to accomplishment and education more evident than in time spent on homework."

Turn the TV Off

This may be one of the hardest things to do for both parents and children. Television is definitely a force to be reckoned with when we're talking about helping children learn the homework habit. According to recent figures, the average child watches 22,000 hours of TV by the time she or he graduates from high school. That's twice as much time as children spend in school.[2]

Between 1978 and 1992, the percentage of American youngsters spending three or more hours a day watching TV jumped dramatically:[3] the percentage of nine-year-olds who watched three to five hours a day of TV increased from 29 percent in

1982 to 41 percent in 1992; from 1978 to 1992 the percentage of thirteen-year-olds increased from 39 to 51 percent, and the percentage of seventeen-year-olds increased from 26 to 40 percent. School achievement "tended to fall" for all three ages as the amount of television viewing went up.

The most eloquent, convincing treatment we've seen of TV's negative effect on kids and families is Jim Trelease's chapter about television in *The Read-Aloud Handbook.*[4] He gives sixteen compelling reasons that TV is not helpful – and sometimes even harmful – to kids. He describes why he and his wife decided to turn off the TV on school nights.

Trelease's children reacted strongly to the decision to shut off the TV. They cried at first. They couldn't envision their evenings without the television. They had a lot of trouble adjusting to the change. Making the change took courage and conviction, but Trelease and his wife stuck it out. In the end, he describes the benefits for his whole family – they started to do things they never had time for before, like doing homework, reading, playing games, and, best of all, talking to one another.

Many of the parents we have spoken with report that they allow no TV on school nights. One father said, "We keep it off so our children will learn to do other things. I have to get my news from newspapers and magazines now. But I don't mind because it's very important to us that our children not watch TV during the school week. My son has read over 500 books and he's only in fourth grade. Turning the TV off has tremendous benefits."

The truth is, we parents need to deal effectively and decisively with television if we are serious about our children's education. This may mean limiting our own use of it, and it certainly means being willing to put helping with homework ahead of our TV watching. It's clear that parents need to put TV into perspective – firmly behind schoolwork – and keep it there!

Ignore Failure, Celebrate Progress

Besides giving efforts to learn their full attention, parents do two other things to encourage efforts when children are young. They ignore failures or unsuccessful attempts, and they celebrate the smallest progress. These elements are also essential for encouraging children to do their homework night after night.

One of the most common complaints we hear from parents is that they lose patience in working with their children. This most often comes from expecting too much too soon. When you give your attention to schoolwork, you have to avoid the pitfall of being overly critical and demanding results right away. This is actually negative attention and will squelch effort – the opposite of what you're trying to do.

You know now that the goal is habit, developing the habit of doing the work – not perfectly, not neatly at first, just the habit of doing it. You don't want to make an issue or a battle out of everything to do with homework. In fact, you want to choose issues carefully. When you taught the child to talk, you were happy in the beginning with "waller." Later on you expected "water," and eventually, "I'd like a glass of water, please." In the beginning, efforts in the right direction were enough. The same is true with schoolwork.

Get them to do the work. When they are doing all their work, they will naturally want to do the work better and more neatly. Gradually they'll even want better grades. In time, these other issues take care of themselves, if the child is doing the work. But for many of us, this is a hard principle to accept and harder still to remember, to hold on to.

One mother was so bothered by her son's lack of neatness that she was blind to the progress he had made. She said, "I just can't work with him. I get mad that he's so sloppy. Then he gets mad and won't do anything."

By focusing on his progress, she was able to stop being overly critical. And he had made considerable progress. He had gone from completing one set of math worksheets twice a week to completing all his work – a set every day. He had even remembered to record the time it took to do the problems.

With some prompting, this mother began to see that her son had improved, and she saw that it was important for her to recognize those improvements. Starting the next week, this mother tried ignoring the things that were "wrong" with her son's work and applauding what he had done well. Slowly he began not only to finish all his worksheets but also to score 100 percent on them – instead of 70 or 80 percent.

That's the process we're looking for. Children who do their work will, over time, eventually correct themselves or accept correction. They will begin to ask, "Why am I getting a C on this? What can I do to improve it?" Neatness, accuracy, and improved performance will come to children who form the habit of doing their work.

This is so important that it needs repeating: First, just get the child to do the work. Other qualities will come, in time, out of the habit of completing work Get your children to do their work and then give them a lot of honest, positive feedback: "I'm proud of you. You've done all this work. Look at what you're learning. You're learning to do all these things."

Emphasize what children get right and forget what seems wrong. A famous book on business management puts it like this: "Try to catch them doing something right!"[5] Our successes are more useful than our failures. All too often from our failures we learn to fail, but from our successes, we learn to succeed.

At first, you just want the work done, and you have to lead the child to that. It takes patience and vision, but you have to trust that neatness, speed, comfort, and good grades will all come eventually if the child does it often enough and for a long enough time. This also applies to grades. As we mentioned in Chapter 4, if you define success in terms of efforts, the grades will come. If you define success in terms of grades, efforts are likely to stop. We want our children to build positive feelings about doing their schoolwork and a sense that they can do it.

Helping children form the homework habit is a gradual process. Children don't learn to run overnight. Most won't quickly learn to work in school. While they're learning, it's helpful to view success in terms of repeated efforts and completed work.

Other Homework Issues

When parents decide to become involved with children's homework, some basic nuts-and-bolts issues always arise.

Finding Out What the Homework Is

A complaint we regularly hear from parents is that their children tell them that they have no homework when they actually do. This is a basic problem. How can parents find out what's going on at school? How can they help their children keep track of their assignments so they can actually do their work?

It's a good idea for youngsters to have a notebook or calendar to write their daily homework assignments in. But just having a place to write down assignments is not the main issue. Actually there are two problems here: one, the child must be willing to write down assignments, and two, he or she must remember to write them down. Here are some suggestions:

1. *Buddy system.* One seventh grader we knew didn't write his homework down in the beginning because he didn't intend to do it. So when his mother convinced him to start working, he had trouble remembering to write down the assignments. The boy's solution was to find a friend in each class – a buddy – to remind him to write down the homework at the same time the friend recorded it. In this way, the seventh grader gradually got into the habit of keeping track of assignments.

2. *Teacher/counselor initialing of homework.* The teacher or counselor indicates that the student has written down the correct homework assignment by putting her or his initials next to the assignment. This is a practice in some schools. Other schools will help you monitor homework in other ways. Some schools even send home weekly or biweekly homework lists. If your school doesn't do this, ask the teacher to consider it.

3. *Telephone numbers of other students.* Because students forget to write down homework consistently and because of absences, it's a good idea for your child to get the telephone numbers of at least two students in each class. Have your son or daughter do this at the beginning of the school year. That way there's someone to call when homework assignments are forgotten.

Some schools emphasize communication. Some even have homework hot lines that parents or students can call. Some teachers call parents regularly or have devised other systems. If you're lucky enough to have one of these services – great! If not, you'll want to set up a system that will work until habit comes into play.

Not Doing the Work for Them

Helping children with their work doesn't mean doing it for them. You may have seen the cartoon where the boy comes running into his dad and says, "Dad, could you help Mom with my homework right now? My favorite TV program's coming on!" Many schools are so wary of this kind of help that they put out strong messages that parents should not be involved at all in homework.

Don't be afraid to get involved. Just be aware of the need to walk the line between helping and doing the work. The idea is to get children into the habit of doing their own work with a parent there to give support and help as needed.

In helping with homework, it's easy to step over the line and do too much. If you do, you can just step back. Marsha remembers when her mother showed her how to combine short, choppy sentences into longer, smoother ones. In the beginning, she would go to her mother every time she had a writing assignment. She would sit back and watch while her mother combined sentences for her. Then her mother caught on and stepped back, turning the writing over to Marsha. "I don't think your English teacher is interested in how well I can write," she said. "You can do it for yourself now."

Independence and Competence

An overemphasis on independence can be a big stumbling block for parents. Recently, a mother called about her son. It seems that he had done very well in school through fifth grade. Starting in sixth grade, on the advice of the guidance counselor, the boy's parents decided that their son needed to become independent. "Let him learn to be responsible. Let him learn the consequences of his actions," they were told, and it seemed like a good idea.

So the parents pulled their support away from their son, telling him that he was to learn to be responsible and independent. The boy became independent, but he began to do poorly and actually failed several subjects.

By the time we were called for tutoring, everyone involved had gotten used to the idea of the boy going it alone. The father didn't want to become involved again. The mother didn't know what to do. The boy didn't want the parents involved. He wanted to be independent, but his skills and work habits were not developed enough for that. The mother said that being independent was kind of a good deal for him, because he knew that he was getting away with a lot. He wasn't doing much in school and wasn't concerned about his grades. Now the family wanted to bring in a tutor to solve the problem. Their son was independent, but he wasn't competent.

Many of us, both parents and teachers, have a real fixation on or infatuation with independence. Maybe it's because we imagine that competent, confident students are independent early in their school lives. Those who really know, know that students often need support throughout most of their school careers. One high school principal of a recognized school of excellence sends home a letter with honor roll students that says: "Please accept our congratulations. We know that students can achieve high scholarship only with the active participation and encouragement of their parents."

When we were teaching at the International School of Islamabad, we knew a couple whose daughter was a top student. They had been in close touch with their daughter and her schoolwork for years. The year that she was in Marsha's eleventh-grade honors American literature class, her father stopped by during a parent-teacher conference day. After looking at and discussing a few of his daughter's papers, he said, "You know, this is the first time I haven't been involved in helping her in some way with her papers – talking through ideas, getting her started."

Their daughter had become both independent and competent, but the competence had come first, and her parents had been significantly involved for all her previous school years. Independence with competence takes time.

Leading Them to Independence

Becoming independent is gradual. Parents first need to lead children to success in their work – by guiding them, by showing them how to do it, and by giving their support. Then let them move toward independence. Ideally, children will gradually take on more and more independence as working becomes habitual, as they become skilled, and as they realize that they can be successful at it. The following are some examples of ways parents can begin to gradually wean youngsters away from an intense need for parents' attention.

One mother reported that her son would do math problems only if she sat with him and watched him work. She started him toward independence by saying, "I have to go to the basement for a minute. Why don't you do this one problem? I'll check it when I get back." In this way, she soon had the boy doing three problems alone, then five, and eventually whole sets of problems independently.

A single father told how his son Freddy gradually overcame severe reading problems and became a more independent reader. In the beginning, Freddy could sustain reading aloud through only one paragraph. So the father would read a paragraph aloud, and then his son would read one. Gradually, he increased the amount his son read. Within a few days, Freddy could read a page at a time, and within two weeks, he could read two pages.

His father kept gradually stretching the boy's reading and pulling himself out of the reading so that his son could eventually read an entire chapter all alone. While the child read, his father verbally encouraged him, saying things like, "Yes! Good reading. You're doing great. Keep going." Working in this way, Freddy was soon at the top of his reading group and was becoming an independent reader.

Patrice, a sixth grader who hated reading, got used to having her mother read a chapter of her required novel to her each night. Then her mother began reading one page and letting Patrice read a page of the novel. Gradually, Patrice was reading more pages of the chapter than her mother was. Halfway through the book, Patrice's mom reported that her daughter was reading the assigned chapters all by herself. And she did well on the chapter quizzes.

A Final Note

When you taught your children to walk and talk, you gave their efforts your full, positive attention. You knew what they were to learn, and you knew your role in their work. You were not in a hurry for results – you knew that they would come eventually. You gave no importance to failures and celebrated the least progress.

This is also the recipe for success with schoolwork, and you can start tonight. All you have to do is clear the dining room table, turn off the TV, and get started.

Strategies
Tools for Effective Study

- Mnemonics: Retaining Information Easily

- Time Management: Making the Most of Study Time

- Interest Management: Liking the Work You Have to Do

- Reading and Math: Two Helpful Programs

Strategy A
Mnemonics
Retaining Information Easily

Thirty days hath September, April, June, and November" and "Every Good Boy Does Fine" are devices many of us have used to remember the number of days in each month and the lines of the treble clef (E, G, B, D, F). These are both examples of mnemonics.

Although the word *mnemonic* sounds technical, it has a simple meaning: something that reminds, a memory aid. And it's a much broader term than most of us think. A string around the finger is a mnemonic because it reminds. When preschool children learn the alphabet to the tune of "Twinkle, Twinkle Little Star," the tune is an aid to memory. As you'll see, some mnemonics use word play and are primarily verbal, like Every Good Boy Does Fine. But the most effective and memorable devices involve the imagination through mental pictures and images.

Some of the best students naturally use mnemonics to remember facts and concepts in school. For example, in *The Memory Book,* Jerry Lucas, a former All-American and All-Pro basketball player, tells how effective and time-saving mnemonics were for him at Ohio State University. In his first class at Ohio State, Lucas's American history professor warned that athletes would have to earn their grades. Lucas was determined to do well and decided to use some of the memory techniques he had developed earlier in his school career. On the first test in American history, he made the highest grade, a 99 – the next highest grade was a 77. Four years later, Lucas graduated Phi Beta Kappa, "having put in something like one-fourth the study time that most students used," largely because of mnemonics.[1]

Just as there are some students, like Jerry Lucas, who naturally or accidentally begin to use mnemonics, there are many other students who struggle in school and don't know about mnemonics. They don't realize that mnemonics can make schoolwork a lot easier. Here we give many examples of mnemonics that are useful for schoolwork and some theory behind why they work. There are also tips on how parents and children can make up their own mnemonics and apply them to different school subjects.

A Few Examples of Mnemonics

A student might remember the number of humps on the two types of camels, Dromedary and Bactrian, by the number of humps in the first letters, D and B. A Dromedary has one hump and a Bactrian two.[2]

To solve the problem $6 + 3 \times 2 - (8 \div 4) = ?$ a student would have to know the *order of operations* in math: **p**arentheses, **e**xponents, **m**ultiplication/**d**ivision, **a**ddition/**s**ubtraction. Math teachers often give students the mnemonic PEMDAS, or **P**lease **E**xcuse **M**y **D**ear **A**unt **S**ally, for remembering the order of operations.

When you learned the names of the Great Lakes in school – **H**uron, **O**ntario, **M**ichigan, **E**rie, **S**uperior – you may have used the mnemonic HOMES. A vivid, colorful image may help make a mnemonic even more memorable. For instance, you might remember HOMES for the Great Lakes more easily if you picture a group of homes floating on the Great Lakes on the map. Or picture the Great Lakes flooding through your home or your neighbor's home.

Although computers are changing this, in the past, medical students were well known for having to commit to memory vast amounts of information. A medical missionary we met in India said that without mnemonics he would never have become a doctor. Another doctor told us that maybe half his class in medical school used and benefited from mnemonics. He said that the students liked mnemonics because many of them were "pretty bawdy."

Here's an example of a popular mnemonic used to learn the names of the nerves, in order, that go through the superior orbital tissues in the skull (**l**acrimal, **f**rontal, **t**rochlear, **l**ateral, **n**asociliary, **i**nternal, **a**bducens): **L**azy **F**rench **T**arts **L**ie **N**aked **I**n **A**nticipation."[3] Of course, this mnemonic also brings to mind an image that's easy to recall.

Why Do Mnemonics Work?

You might find yourself thinking, it takes time to think up these things, these mnemonics, so wouldn't my youngster's time be better spent learning the material itself? A number of students have raised this same objection. The time spent creating mnemonics is time well spent, however, if they work for your child: first, a well-constructed mnemonic is easily remembered, so students don't waste time relearning material; second, after students become skilled at coming up with them, mnemonics can save a great deal of study time, as Jerry Lucas discovered in college.

Mnemonics work for several reasons. When you use them:

1. *You are using the information to be learned.*
   When you make a mnemonic, you *use* the study material. You play with it, manipulate it, make personal associations, "own" it in a sense. Maybe that's why it's said that the best remembered mnemonics are those you make up for yourself.[4]

2. *You are involving the visual, imaginative part of the mind.*
   Vivid, absurd pictures appeal to the imagination. In fact, many of the elements of mnemonics – pictures and images, stories, rhyme and rhythm, melody – involve the right hemisphere of the brain.[5] That's one of the reasons mnemonics work so well – the imaginative, musical, emotional part of the mind as well as the more verbal, logical part is at work. The *whole* mind is more completely involved in learning. One researcher reports that "the Greeks realized that in order to remember well, you have to use every aspect of your mind."[6]

3. *You are making the study material more important.*
   Through mnemonics, information takes on more significance, which is one of the keys to remembering. We remember events that have great significance. Ask anyone old enough to remember the assassinations of John F. Kennedy or Martin Luther King, and they will probably be able to tell you in some detail where they were, what they were doing, and how they felt. The significance of the event imprinted the details in their memories.

How To Make Up Your Own Mnemonics

We've found from experience that simple mnemonics are best for schoolwork. The easiest to get started on are absurd sentences or words (acronyms) made from the first letters of key words and terms to be remembered. And those sentences or acronyms are remembered more easily if they bring to mind crazy, absurd images.

For example, a biology student at the Karachi American School learned the kingdoms – **P**rotista, **M**onera, **F**ungi, **P**lantae, **A**nimalea – with this crude but memorable sentence and image: **P**rotesting **M**onks **F**arted **P**lants and **A**nimals. He used the first letters of the kingdoms to create this colorful sentence and a mental picture of monks carrying protest signs and leaving a trail of cloudy, smelly plants and animals wherever they walked to help remember it.

Absurd? Humorous? Exaggerated? Coarse? Yes! Those are the kinds of images that appeal most to the imagination, so they are the most easily remembered. The ancient Romans were on to this idea 3,000 years ago, as shown in the scrolls called *Ad Herennium*:

> When we see in everyday life things that are petty, ordinary, and banal, we generally fail to remember them, because the mind is not being stirred by anything novel or marvelous. But if we see or hear something exceptionally base, dishonorable, unusual, great, unbelievable, or ridiculous, that we are likely to remember for a long time.[7]

Present-day memory experts say the same thing: the images or mental pictures that are best remembered are unusual or exaggerated, sensual or colorful, active or moving, vulgar or sexual, absurd or ridiculous. If we make our pictures too logical, they become ordinary and forgettable. So instead of putting a shoe on a foot where it logically belongs, put it on a head or in a mouth, places it doesn't logically belong. And make the shoe enormous or tiny.

In the beginning, you may think that you have to create slick, perfect mnemonics, the kind often published in books. The truth is, study material may not lend itself to simple, elegant mnemonics like HOMES for the Great Lakes. Most mnemonics are silly and personal, with lots of rough edges. The idea is to find one quickly that works.

The key points to remember are:

- Most mnemonics are scruffy and crude – not elegant, orderly, and slick.

- The images most easily remembered are:
    exaggerated
    absurd
    vulgar
    colorful
    moving
    active
    ridiculous

- Students remember best the mnemonics they make up for themselves.

- Simple mnemonics are the best and most useful for school-work: Absurd sentences or words (acronyms) containing the first letters of the key words or terms tend to be remembered best (like the example above for remembering kingdoms). Sound-alike associations (see the "vocabulary" examples below) or crazy stories that students can "walk through" mentally are also useful.

Mnemonics Applied to Several Study Areas

Social Studies and History (Middle School or Upper Elementary)

For a social studies class in Karachi, students had to learn the names and attributes of one goddess and several gods worshipped in ancient Egypt.

Ra	the sun god
Osiris	god of the Nile, fertility, underworld
Isis	sister and wife of Osiris, goddess of the moon and of protection
Horus	son of Osiris and Isis, god of the sky

One of the students made up the following story to remember this information. As you read, try to picture vividly each event that takes place. The images identify the areas of life these gods are associated with. Even though this fantasy may seem long, remember that images travel through the mind quickly and are a powerful aid to memory.

Imagine entering an ancient Egyptian place of worship. You're startled to see a bunch of sunburned cheerleaders looking up at the sun and leading a cheer. You hear them shout "Ra! Ra! Ra!" (Ra is the sun god.) Next you notice the letters, O-H-I-O, on the cheerleaders' sweaters. The first three letters, O-H-I, stand for the names of the members of an important family of gods: Osiris, his wife Isis, and their son Horus.

Diving through the "O" on one cheerleader's sweater, you find yourself swimming in the Nile River with Osiris, the god of the Nile. Osiris sprinkles a handful of water on the riverbank, and wheat and corn spring up immediately, for he's the god of fertility. But then the wheat and corn turn just as quickly into pale ghosts, sighing, "Oh, si(r) us," and you remember that Osiris is also the god of the underworld.

You look again at the cheerleader's sweater and see that the "H" has become a ladder. You climb the "H" up into the sky where a huge horse (Horus) is flying around you. Horus is the god of the sky.

Looking back at the cheerleader's sweater, you see the "I" turn into an eye and then into the moon, for Isis is the goddess of the moon. (You could as easily have her turn around and display her bare bottom – or "moon" you – and in that way remember that she's the "moon" goddess.) The moon goddess immediately whips out an insurance policy and tries to sell it to you. Remember, she's also the goddess of protection!

If you've vividly imagined this fantasy, it should trigger your memory of the images and the information they contain. Close your eyes and see if you can go back through the story. See if you can remember the gods and the information about them.

American History (High School)

Mnemonics are particuarly well suited to remembering lists. In American history, students often have to learn the two groups of states that opposed each other over signing the Articles of Confederation, the document that joined the thirteen original states before the Constitution was drawn up.

This dispute revolved around land. On one side were seven states claiming land in the western territories. On the other side were six states with no claim to western land and thus no expansionist possibilities. Here's one way to put the first letters of each group of states into silly sentences that suggest ridiculous images and help you remember the states in each group:

For the seven states with land claims that favored the Articles (Connecticut, New York, Georgia, Virginia, Massachusetts, South Carolina, North Carolina): **ConNY GaVe Ma a SCuNC** (skunk). Picture a girl named Conny presenting your mother with a skunk. To make the image pungent, smell the skunk, see your Ma recoil at that smell.

For the six states that initially opposed the Articles (Pennsylvania, Maryland, New Hampshire, New Jersey, Rhode Island, Delaware): **PENNy Makes NEW HAM** from **NEW J**uicy **R**ooster **D**roppings. Picture someone named Penny picking up rooster droppings and molding them into a ham. Make the image vivid.

Vocabulary (English, Science, Foreign Language)

Mnemonics are great for remembering vocabulary in all subjects, but especially for English and foreign languages, because generally there are so many *more* words to learn in those subjects.

A mnemonic makes remembering the Hindi word *nuhair,* meaning "large, man-made canal" easy. *Nuhair* is pronounced a little like "no hair," so we picture a bald man (because the word is masculine) standing in a huge, water-filled canal throwing water on his head.

Here are some ways to find associations for vocabulary:

* use the sound of the entire vocabulary word

* use the sound of part of the word

* use the spelling of the word or a combination of spelling and sound

Try making up a mnemonic for a word with an abstract meaning – for example, *cursory,* meaning hasty, superficial. Take a few minutes to make an association for the word and see what comes to mind. What does the word sound like? What does it remind you of? Make a crazy association. Make a crazy image. Make the association – the mnemonic – absurd, dumb, colorful, vulgar. Let yourself go. Tie the meaning of the word to the sound of the word in the mnemonic.

Here are the three different approaches applied to the word *cursory*:

1. Focus on the entire word. It sounds like "curse her e." Imagine a friend who writes such *hasty* *e*'s that her notes are unreadable. Whenever you get a note from her, you find yourself saying, "Curse her *e*!"

2. Give your attention to part of the word. *Cursory* contains *cursor*, which marks where you are on a computer or word processor. Imagine an enormous, speeding cursor on your word processor – one that jumps around so fast that it causes you to make *hasty*, cursory mistakes.

3. Use the spelling: C-U-R-SORY (see, you are sorry). Imagine you are washing dishes so hastily and so negligently that you break half of them and leave the surviving half filthy. See the mess your *hasty*, cursory work leaves. "See, you are sorry" (c-u-r-sory).

In all three examples, images are used to tie together the word and its somewhat abstract meaning.

But a mnemonic may trigger an image or it may not. For example, here are mnemonics without images for two other words, *lax* and *eccentric*. They aren't elegant, but they can help you remember.

• lax (adjective) means slack or negligent. *Lax* is contained in the word *relax*, so remember that you can be so relaxed that you forget the *re* and use only the *lax*. That's pretty slack and negligent!

• eccentric (adjective) means strange, odd, unconventional. Use the last four letters as a reminder that this *tric* is one of the *strangest* tricks you'll see: it's spelled without a k.

Metric Distances for Math and Chemistry (Elementary, Middle, and High School)

Here's a mnemonic that a seventh grader came up with for learning metric lengths and distances: **K**ing **H**enry **D**rank **M**y **D**irty **C**ement **M**ixer.

King	Henry	Drank	My	Dirty	Cement	Mixer
Kilometer	Hectometer	Dekameter	Meter	Decimeter	Centimeter	Millimeter

This mnemonic becomes memorable if you picture it. Picture King Henry. See him pick up an incredibly dirty and enormous cement mixer and drink it, truck and all. Of course, the mixer will have to liquefy as he drinks it. Or have King Henry pick up the cement mixer and see it become tiny – small enough to dissolve in a glass of water. In that case, see Henry drop the mixer in the glass of water and drink the water and the cement mixer and maybe the glass as well. Close your eyes and imagine either image vividly, then go on.

If the mnemonic worked, you should be able to write down the first letter of each word in order. Try it.

— — — — — — —

What's especially useful about this mnemonic is that it can be used to *convert* metric lengths, another thing math students have to learn.

Extended a bit, this conversion is also useful in high school chemistry. This is the formula given in some chemistry textbooks:

$$\frac{100 \text{ cm}}{100 \text{ cm}} = \frac{1 \text{ m}}{100 \text{ cm}} \quad \textit{simplifies to} \quad 1 = \frac{1 \text{ m}}{100 \text{ cm}}$$

$$45 \text{ cm} \times 1 = 45 \text{ cm} \times \frac{1 \text{ m}}{100 \text{ cm}} \quad \textit{simplifies to} \quad 45 = \frac{45 \text{ m}}{100 \text{ cm}}$$

$$45 \text{ cm} = 45 \text{ m} \div 100 \text{ cm} \quad \textit{gives the answer} \quad 45 \text{ cm} = 0.45 \text{ m}$$

It's much easier to use the mnemonic **King Henry Drank My Dirty Cement Mixer** to convert distances. Here's how you do it for converting 21 meters and 21.6 meters, first to centimeters and then to kilometers:

Step 1: Plug in the numbers so that the number with the decimal point to its right is beneath the distance you're dealing with. Remember that a decimal point is understood in every number whether you see it or not. The decimal point is obvious in 21.6 meters but left out of 21 meters, where it is understood to be after the right-most number (i.e., 21.0). So for both 21.0 and 21.6 meters, put the 1 under the M for meters.

Step 2: Put zeros under all the other distances. At first this may help with converting distances – later you won't need to do this.

Step 3: Move the decimal point to the right of the number (or zero) beneath the distance you're converting to. In the first case, the distance is centimeters, so the decimal point would go to the right of the number under the C.

Converting from Meters to Centimeters

Step 1: Plug in the numbers

K	H	D	M	D	C	M		K	H	D	M	D	C	M
			2	1.	0						2	1.	6	

Step 2: Add zeros under all the other distances

K	H	D	M	D	C	M		K	H	D	M	D	C	M
0	0	2	1.	0	0	0		0	0	2	1.	6	0	0

Step 3: Move the decimal point

K	H	D	M	D	C	M		K	H	D	M	D	C	M
0	0	2	1	0	0.	0		0	0	2	1	6	0.	0

21 m = 2,100 cm   21.6 m = 2,160 cm

Converting from Meters to Kilometers

Step 1: Plug in the numbers

K	H	D	M	D	C	M		K	H	D	M	D	C	M
			2	1.	0						2	1.	6	

Step 2: Add zeros under all the other distances

K	H	D	M	D	C	M		K	H	D	M	D	C	M
0	0	2	1.	0	0	0		0	0	2	1.	6	0	0

Step 3: Move the decimal point

K	H	D	M	D	C	M		K	H	D	M	D	C	M
0.	0	2	1	0	0	0		0.	0	2	1	6	0	0

21 m = 0.021 km   21.6 m = 0.0216 km

If you want to read more about mnemonics, there are a number of books around, including the ones below.

Tony Buzan, *Use Both Sides of Your Brain* (New York: Plume, 1989).

Tony Buzan, *Use Your Perfect Memory* (New York: E.P. Dutton, 1984).

Harry Lorayne, *Super Memory, Super Student* (Boston: Little, Brown, 1990).

Colin Rose, *Accelerated Learning* (New York: Dell Publishing, 1985).

Peter Russell, *The Brain Book* (New York: Hawthorn Books, 1979).

Strategy B
Time Management
Making the Most of Study Time

J ust as there have been numerous studies on ways to increase productivity in the workplace, much research has been done on ways to make learning more productive. Here we introduce study strategies that came from this research – ones that work in harmony with the way the mind works. These particular strategies show how to establish an effective routine for study, and how to structure study time and study material so learning is more productive. Strategies include:

- taking breaks

- "chunking" material

- warm-up

- review

If youngsters make even one or two of these study tools a habit, their learning will be quicker, more efficient, and more enjoyable.

Strategy 1 — Taking Breaks

When we think of intense study, we picture students slogging away for long hours without a break. Actually, research shows that students learn more, learn faster, and study with more intensity if they work *less* continuously and take more breaks. By taking frequent, well-planned rests, they get better results for less work. Study becomes less painful, more relaxed, more productive.

The strategy of taking breaks to increase productivity in industry was tried in the 1940s at Bethlehem Steel. Individual laborers at the company were found to be able to carry and load about twelve and a half tons of pig iron a day. This puzzled Frederick Taylor, a scientific-management engineer for the company. He estimated that workers should be able to handle four times that amount. When he began to study the men's work habits, he soon discovered that they were exhausted every day by noon.

Taylor reasoned that taking regular breaks might increase the laborers' productivity and decided to test this idea. He assigned someone to oversee the work schedule of one laborer, a man named Schmidt. The overseer used a watch to control Schmidt's work time and to make sure that he took regular breaks. In this way, working for only twenty-six minutes each hour and resting for thirty-four minutes, Schmidt was able to carry and load forty-seven tons every day over a period of several months.

The experiment showed that Taylor's estimates were right: workers had the capacity to carry and load about four times the pig iron they had been carrying. He attributed Schmidt's increased productivity to a simple reason, "he rested before he got tired."[1]

Is Studying Like Carrying Pig-Iron?

With studying and learning, the same thing is true: if students work until they're exhausted, they'll accomplish much less than if they take regular breaks. And make no mistake, mental work can be as tiring as physical labor. "In fact, the brain can burn as many calories in intense concentration as the muscles do during exercise. That's why thinking can feel as exhausting as a physical workout."[2]

But studies show that there is another, perhaps more important reason that taking breaks makes learning more effective. Because of the way the mind naturally works, regular breaks or rest periods enable students to *remember* much more of what they study. And this effect has nothing to do with tiredness or with whether a student feels the need for a break.[3]

We first saw the positive effects of this strategy in 1980, when a high school junior at Woodstock School in India asked Jack for help with chemistry during an evening study hall.

Jack was preparing to teach a study skills class for the school and had just read in Tony Buzan's *Use Both Sides of Your Brain*, that taking breaks enhances memory. He told the student, "I've never used it, but a book I'm reading suggests that taking breaks could be just what you're looking for."

The boy was desperate and willing to try anything, so, for an hour and a half that night, he studied in ten- and fifteen-minute sessions and took a short rest period after each session. During study sessions, he worked intensely. During rest periods, he got completely away from work for a couple of minutes – took short walks, went to the water fountain, or just stood and stretched.

About a week later his results came: 92 percent, an A. All his other test grades that quarter had been F's.

Why did the strategy of breaking up study time work so well? Research shows that we remember best what's studied at the *beginning* and *end* of a study session and tend to forget what's studied in the middle – which includes most of the material in a long, unbroken study session.[4] When students take regular breaks, they increase the number of beginnings and endings in a study session. This alone allows them to remember more of what they study, without extra effort.

It's easy to see how it might work if you compare the two charts on the next page. The first depicts the amount of study material remembered from a two-hour study period with no breaks. It shows two peaks of remembering and a valley of forgetting in the middle. The second chart shows that a break taken every twenty minutes over two hours would naturally produce *ten* peaks of remembering rather than two!

Advantages and Applications of Breaks

Taking breaks has a number of advantages:

1. As in the pig-iron study, breaks keep the student from getting fatigued. They allow the mind and body a chance to rest and release built-up tension.

2. Breaks are a way to get better results for less actual effort because they increase the number of peaks of remembering in a study session. Taking four breaks during a two-hour study period increases the peaks of remembering fivefold – from two peaks to ten (see charts on next page).

3. Limiting the length of study sessions allows for more intense concentration. Two hours, an hour and a half, even an hour is an awfully long time to sustain concentration during study.

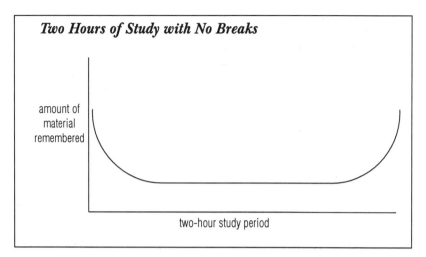

Two Hours of Study with No Breaks

amount of
material
remembered

two-hour study period

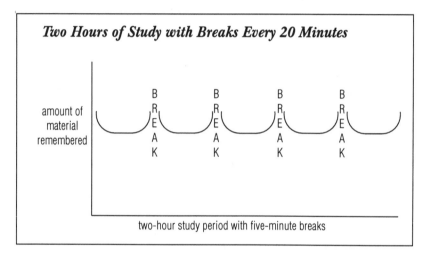

Two Hours of Study with Breaks Every 20 Minutes

amount of
material
remembered

B   B   B   B
R   R   R   R
E   E   E   E
A   A   A   A
K   K   K   K

two-hour study period with five-minute breaks

But it's relatively easy to study intensely for fifteen to twenty minutes at a time.

4. Breaks are a way to take advantage of another effect. Research shows that a learner actually recalls *more* after two to ten minutes of rest than immediately after studying.[5] Some researchers think that this rise in recall comes from the brain's having time to digest and organize information more fully.[6] Students can take advantage of this rise by resting and then coming back to study during the time of high recall. Tony Buzan makes this comment about the rise in recall:

This last piece of information is particularly important because it stops your feeling a little guilty when you find yourself naturally taking a break but at the same time think that you ought to be getting "back to the grindstone."[7]

Taking breaks works well for studying one subject intensively. As part of an experiment on ways to improve learning, one of Marsha's psychology students tried taking breaks as a way to improve her grade in her hardest subject, AP biology. On the Saturday before the final exam, she was able to study for almost eight hours because she took a break every twenty to thirty minutes. During some breaks she lay down, took a few deep breaths, and relaxed. Other times she did affirmations and visualizations. By breaking the work up and resting, she got through that intense study time staying relatively relaxed and absorbing reams of material. Her experiment worked: she made an A on the exam.

Breaks work just as well when there is homework to be done in several subjects. Elementary-age children are not going to have whole nights of homework in one subject. Even high school students often have small amounts of work in several subjects rather than a large amount in one subject.

Here's what a two-hour study session covering two subjects, English and history, might look like:

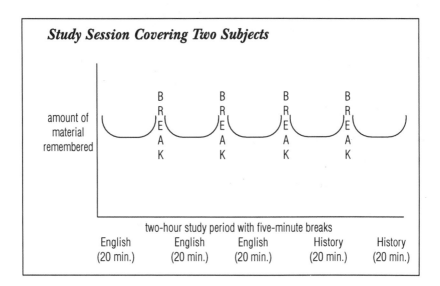

General Advice about Breaking Up Study Sessions

Parents have two roles in making breaks a habit: to introduce the strategy and explain its value, and to help children get started using it. Here are the basics for getting started:

- *Make study sessions ten to thirty minutes in length.*
  Of course, the length can vary with the age of the child – shorter for elementary students and longer for older students. It also varies with the kind of assignment the child is doing. For example, solving math problems might require only ten- to fifteen-minute study sessions, whereas reading a short story might require twenty- to thirty-minute sessions.

- *Make the breaks or rest periods two to ten minutes long.*
  The length of the breaks should correspond to the length of the study sessions – shorter breaks, two minutes, for shorter study sessions (ten- to fifteen-minute ones), and longer breaks, up to ten minutes, for longer study sessions (twenty- to thirty- minute ones).

- *Do "something else" during breaks.*
  Ideal activities take the mind completely off studies. Tony Buzan, in *Use Your Perfect Memory,* recommends allowing the mind to rest by taking a walk, getting something to drink or eat, doing some visualizations, or putting on some music.[8] Children can learn to juggle during breaks. A few minutes of juggling gives a total break from studying and a shift from logic and reasoning to a right-brain activity. Other short, active, right-brained activities work as well.

  For younger children, be aware that they can get easily distracted from studying. They might get a drink of water or juice or bounce a ball against the wall – anything that gives a short, complete rest from the work but allows them to get back to work easily when it's time.

- *Get a timer or clock that can easily be reset.*
  A digital kitchen timer works best. It's very easy to set and, unlike a clock, shows only how much time is left in a study session. For this reason, a timer helps keep the focus on study. Older students can easily set a timer for fifteen or twenty minutes, take a break, and then reset the timer.

- *Take breaks even if study is going well.*
  It's not a question of how they feel – students benefit from taking breaks even if they are not tired and still understand the material being studied.

Strategy 2 — Chunking

The second strategy, *chunking*, is similar to the strategy of taking breaks and can be effectively combined with breaks. Chunking is different in that it has to do with limiting the amount of material to be learned rather than the length of study time.

George Miller of Harvard demonstrated in "The Magical Number Seven, Plus or Minus Two" that our immediate memory is limited to a maximum of about seven items. Miller found that breaking material to be learned into segments that size or smaller made the learning easier. Educators call this "chunking."[9]

For years, the phone company has done a type of chunking with telephone numbers. It found that it was easier for people to remember 268-5710 than 2685710. Even a ten-digit number like 6152685710 is relatively easy to remember when it's chunked, 615-268-5710.

In a narrow sense, chunking has to do with memory – breaking a long list into small pieces to remember the list more easily. Chunking is such a useful concept that we've taken some liberties with it. We've used it in a broader, looser sense to include breaking study material and complicated tasks into small, doable parts or steps – not just for remembering the material, but for doing the tasks more easily as well.

Solving fifteen multiplication problems, learning twenty spelling words in elementary school or twenty-five vocabulary words in high school, putting together a science fair project – all these can seem overwhelming to an inexperienced youngster who hasn't been shown how to chunk. But all these tasks become much more doable and manageable emotionally when chunked or broken into a relatively simple set of steps.

When your daughter comes home with those fifteen multiplication problems in elementary school or fifteen algebra problems in high school, suggest chunking the fifteen problems into groups of five. Have her do the first five problems and then check the answers in the back of the book or, if necessary, call a friend. Checking work after completing each chunk ensures that it's being done correctly.

Chunking the problems allows youngsters to be nearly as fresh on the last problem as they were on the fifth. With more difficult word problems, fewer problems can be put in each chunk of work. With relatively simple computations, more can be put in.

More complex assignments such as book reports and science fair projects also benefit from chunking. They become much more manageable when approached as a series of small steps rather than as something to be done all at once.

In addition to making work simpler and more manageable, chunking gives two other benefits. It allows students to be more intensely involved with smaller amounts of material, and makes it likely that they will do more of the work correctly.

A story about Yo Yo Ma, the renowned cello virtuoso, illustrates the value of chunking in music practice. In an interview, Yo Yo Ma told about being taught in an unusual way when he was very young. The solos he tried were so hard for a pupil his age that to attempt them as a whole would have been overwhelming. So his father gave him one very short segment (only a few notes) of a difficult cello work each week. Yo Yo Ma perfected that one small segment of the large solo as well as he could. The next week he got another one like it to learn and add to the previous segment. This chunking of long, difficult cello works made them approachable both emotionally and technically, because he worked on manageable amounts and learned them correctly and easily.[10]

Strategy 3 — Warm-Ups

Just as athletes benefit from a short warm-up before competing, students benefit from a warm-up before study. Studies show two specific benefits from warm-ups: they create a mental set or preparation for the material that is to be learned, and they increase the ability of the learner to retain or recall the information to be learned.[11]

In one experiment two groups of subjects were given lists of paired adjectives to learn. After twenty-four hours one group was given a short warm-up task before relearning, the other was not. The surprising thing was not that the warm-up group showed better rentention, but that they showed *no forgetting, even improving slightly.*[12]

A warm-up is also a way of easing into work so that it seems less daunting. Students often find it hard to get started on their evening's homework. Like adults, they procrastinate. Homework seems cold and dead, a burdensome task, so they find excuses to put it off. When students actually sit down, look over, and list what they have to do via a warm-up, they often find that the work is much less than they had imagined it to be.

What do children do in a warm-up? Several things: review notes, look over a chapter before reading it, mentally review what was done in class, mentally review the steps for solving a math problem or two.

For elementary-age children, give them a warm-up without explaining it to them by:

- discussing an assignment and what was done in class

- looking over the book, worksheet, or assignment sheet together

- having children explain how to do their work, and helping them find an approach if they don't know how to do it

After children become experienced with warming up through your interest and involvement, tell them of the value of warm-ups and suggest that they do warm-ups at the beginning of study for each subject by:

- thinking through the assignment

- looking over the book, worksheet, or assignment and planning how to approach the work

- answering mentally a few of the questions or mentally going through the steps for solving a problem or two

Middle and high school students can easily do warm-ups alone once they understand what a warm-up is and know its value. Parents will only need to give it their attention occasionally. You can get older students started using warm-ups if you approach them in the same way and with the same interest you would show for the work of younger students. It takes only a few minutes of a parent's time to do what Jack did just the other night with our daughter.

As she pulled out her books at the dining room table, he casually asked, "What are you doing in geometry these days?"

"Let's see," she said. "I have seven problems tonight but no proofs to do, I hope. Oh, no, I guess I have one proof."

"Do you know how to do all these?" her dad asked, looking at the book. "What about this one? How do you solve it?"

Sarah explained a little and they looked over the proof she had to do. In a minute or two the exchange was over. She had done most of the talking, and she was ready to work.

A warm-up can be that simple, and it serves another purpose as well. It's a way for parents to show interest in schoolwork. It doesn't have to happen often for youngsters to know that parents care about their work and are available to help in some way.

Strategy 4 — Review

Let's say your son has just spent two hours studying history. How does he ensure he'll remember what he's learned? Review! Surprisingly, the most important review is the one that comes *just after* a study session.

Most forgetting occurs immediately after learning. It will be seen that even one hour afterward more than half of the original had been forgotten. Nine hours afterward about 60 percent of the original had been lost, and one month afterward 80 percent had gone.[13]

Studies show that a review done two to ten minutes after a study session ensures that the material learned is retained for at least a day.[14] That's why this first review is so important and needs to be a regular part of study. But unfortunately, if your son has just finished studying for a test, he is often unwilling or reluctant to go back and review. He thinks that it's an addition to his study: "I just spent the last two hours studying for a history test, and have other work to do. I know that history chapter now and I don't have time to review it!"

"So," you ask, "how do I get my son to build review into his study schedule?"

Here's an approach that we found effective. Make review a short but regular part of the last study session for that history test, not an additional session. For example, if a student is going to spend two hours studying for a history test, he can break his studying into five twenty-minute sessions with breaks in between. Then at the beginning of his sixth and last session, he can take three to five minutes to review what he's already studied. That way, he'll get a review, but it won't seem like something extra. This review still takes place a few minutes after the five previous study sessions.

For example, when children are preparing for a test on the 6's multiplication table in math, they can study in several ten- to fifteen-minute sessions with breaks in between. Then, as they begin the third and final session, you could remind them to go over the material for three to five minutes before going on to assignments in other subjects.

Students may find it helpful to do another short review the following morning, after sleep has allowed the information to be digested. This second review is helpful, easy to do, and consistent with research on review.[15]

As with the other strategies, parents have two roles to play. First, you introduce the concept of review and explain the importance of doing a three- to five-minute review at the beginning of the last study session. Second, you help your child get started using review. If you have the time to get involved, you can help the review process by showing interest in the work, and asking questions about it after it's finished.

Interest Management
Liking the Work You Have to Do

Think about your own experiences in school, on the job, and at home. If you like a subject, task, or project and feel that you're competent in that area, you're much more likely to work well and effectively. With something you don't like and don't think you're good at, you're far more likely to avoid the work and to perform it less competently. The same is true for children. Their performance is powerfully shaped by experiences and how those experiences make them feel.

A third grader finishes a set of math problems and turns them in. The teacher gives the work back and says, "This is wonderful! You got them all right. That's 100 percent, an A." How will this child feel the next time she sits down to do a math assignment? What will she say about math and herself?

It's likely that she will feel great. And there's a good chance that she will say to herself things like, "This math stuff is all right. Let me do some more of it." The student performs well on more tests and quizzes until she eventually takes home an A in math on her report card, with the comment, "Great work!" Let this sort of performance go on for several years, and you'll have a student who enjoys math, is competent in it, and is willing to work.

The same girl gets a spelling test back and the teacher shakes her head and says, "You must not have studied; you did very poorly. You missed ten words." The paper is marked F. That night the teacher sends a note home, "Needs help with spelling!" Soon the report card reflects the student's poor spelling work. Let this sort of performance go on for several years and you'll have a student who dislikes spelling, believes she can't spell, and is unwilling to devote much time or effort to it.

When you try to get your children into the habit of doing homework, you'll find out how important their feelings are. Like Andrew in Chapter 7, most children easily ignore work in subjects they don't like. But when students like a subject and feel that they are "good" at it, they're more likely to work and more likely to do well.

So learning to manage their interest in or liking for school subjects can be a key to students' working hard. As parents, we can help children change the way they feel about a school subject or about doing homework in that subject. We can show children how to begin to like and take an interest in a disliked subject — and out of that interest their performance may begin to improve.

But how do you like something you really don't like? Students can use the same tools we recommended in Chapter 6 for parents to change their beliefs about their children — visualization (imagination) and self-talk (affirmations). We don't have to leave this to chance. Students can learn to use their imaginations and what they say to themselves to change how they feel about a subject and about their performance in it.

Making Self-Talk Positive and Conscious

The experience of a seventh-grade math student of Jack's at the Karachi American School provides a good example of the power of self-talk. At the end of the second marking period, the girl's parents complained, "Mary is making B's, and she made B's last year in math. Yet she scores in the 98th percentile in math on her achievement tests. What's going on? She should be making A's. Why is she doing this?"

Jack told them he wasn't sure, but that she constantly said all sorts of negative things about herself and about math. He described how she entered the class with a litany of negative self-talk: "I had a horrible time with that homework. It was so hard. I took an hour to finish it all. I'm terrible at math. I hate it." The girl's parents said that they had heard the same things at home.

When they called their daughter in to join their conference, she said that she didn't realize how many negative things she had said about math and about herself. As an experiment, Mary agreed to try making only positive statements for a while.

In the beginning, she joked, sarcastically saying things like, "Oh, I really loved that math homework last night!" But gradually she stopped making negative statements and replaced them with truly positive ones. Interestingly, this happened in the third quarter, when most students had trouble maintaining their averages because the work was harder. While many saw their grades fall that quarter, Mary's went up to an A.

We've found that students often balk at saying positive things to themselves about something they know they don't like and don't feel good about. They often say, "You want me to lie to myself! This sounds like brainwashing!"

The truth is, in a real sense, they are already brainwashed. By repeating negative things about a subject, they have convinced themselves that they're not good at the subject or that they can't do the work. By repeating strongly negative messages about themselves and the subject, students often limit their performance and their willingness to work. Like Mary, they're not aware of what they are doing.

So when students say, "You want me to lie to myself," our reply is: "You're already saying things to yourself, negative things. Why not say positive things instead? Why not use this same habit of the mind consciously and positively?"

Using the Imagination Positively

It was a week before Woodstock School's senior music recital – an important event. One senior we knew had had a number of traumatic performance experiences, breaking down on stage, unable to finish solos, falling apart in auditions and other stressful situations. As the recital drew nearer, her imagination replayed those past experiences over and over – and her playing became worse and worse. In the words of her flute teacher, "She could play this solo a week ago, but she's so nervous now that she can't play it anymore."

The girl said that the recital date was a "black hole" on her mental calendar, and she didn't know how to deal with it. Her previous experiences were overwhelming her emotionally. She needed a way to have some positive performance experiences.

Positive use of the imagination was that way. The girl decided to practice, several times a day, how she wanted to feel before and during the upcoming performance. She imagined herself outside the school's auditorium in her black crepe dress, flute in hand, and she practiced how she wanted to feel.

She imagined being calm, confident, and relaxed. In her imagination, she opened the door, entered the hall, and put the music on the stand – all the while keeping her focus, staying relaxed yet determined. She imagined keeping that focus into and throughout her playing. She did this exercise many times.

After two days, the girl's flute teacher reported that she could play the concerto quite well again, and she continued to play it well, right through the senior rectial. The student later said that she must have done the imagination exercise a hundred times that week. That's how desperate she was.

We've seen this technique help with test jitters in the same way. As a senior in high school, Daniel used visualization to change his feelings about taking the SAT. He had already taken an SAT prep course, but because of nervousness, he had made a low score on the exam. Daniel attended three one-hour tutoring sessions during which he learned to practice how he wanted to feel during the actual test.

Using his imagination, he mentally put himself in the stressful test situation and practiced feeling calm, concentrated, and positive, in much the same way as the flute student had done. By focusing on how he wanted to feel during the test, he was able to become *experienced* in a positive way through his imagination. The student wrote:

Not only did it improve my score on the verbal section 150 points, I was able to apply what I learned to soccer and basketball. The mental prep I learned helped me to relax before games and it improved my performance considerably. Not only can it help on the SAT, but in everyday life.

These two techniques – visualization and self-talk – can help people deal effectively with stress. Students can also use the exercises to change how they feel about a subject or task, or how they feel about doing homework and classwork. We call this "interest management."

Changing Feelings about School Subjects

When we were teaching at the International School of Islamabad, a number of students in Marsha's twelfth-grade psychology class did an experiment to see if changing their interest in subjects they didn't like could raise their grades. In the beginning, some of them were extremely skeptical. One boy said, "I can't even imagine being excited about doing my calculus homework." Everyone laughed because that was exactly the point of the experiment – to be able to imagine liking subjects.

The seniors used imagination and self-talk to change the way they felt about one subject they disliked or were uninterested in. At the end of the three-week experiment, they described the strategies they had used daily and reported their grades in the chosen class. All but one student reported a marked improvement not only in the grade but also in their enjoyment of the subject. Here's what three students had to say about their experiment:

Pam wrote on the first day: "Not only is calculus hard to understand, it is hard to like. No matter what I do, I can't seem to get the hang of it." Though she wanted to do her work, she felt conflict because she didn't enjoy it.

After several weeks of using both self-talk and imagination to change her interest and feelings, Pam reported improved grades and wrote: "The techniques were simple enough that I didn't feel that I had to force myself to do what I wanted. . . . Now calculus is actually fun."

Adele also used both techniques. She wrote: "My grade in French for the first quarter was a B; now it is an A! I achieved what my goal was. . . . But I not only raised my grade in French, I also enjoy the language. . . . For me, doing French now has become more of a pleasure than before. My attitude toward the language is extremely positive."

Another senior related: "When I received my progress report in chemistry for the second quarter, I had a total of 54 percent, an F. It was the same day I started my project. Three weeks later my teacher put up another progress report and I have a C–. I couldn't believe it. Surely he must have mixed up the numbers, but there it was."

This student said that she had used relaxation and visualization and then had said certain affirmations over and over: "I love chemistry. Chemistry is fun. I understand my homework. Doing the formulas is like a game." Within one week she reported finding herself wanting to finish her other homework so she could do her chemistry. She came to see it almost as a reward, something she could do when all her other homework was over. She said, "It helped me improve in my other subjects as well during this three-week session."

The Two Techniques Described

We have written what follows as if it were for the person actually using the techniques. Parents can read this section and explain it to their children or have the children read it for themselves.

Before doing both visualization and self-talk, it's helpful to do a little relaxation and deep breathing. Find a comfortable place to sit or lie down. Take a few deep breaths and relax.

Visualization, or Positive Use of the Imagination

Shut your eyes so you aren't distracted by anything around you. A good place to begin is to think of an area, a subject, or an activity that you do very well, that you feel very confident in, that you enjoy doing. It could be a sport like football or basketball, a subject in school like science or English, or an activity like playing a musical instrument.

Imagine that you are doing that activity. Then recall how you feel when you're involved in it. Come up with some adjectives that describe those feelings. One SAT class came up with this list:

- I feel confident.

- I feel relaxed and calm.

- I enjoy the activity.

- I feel aggressive.

- I know I'll do well at it.

These are the kinds of feelings most of have when we do something we're good at and enjoy doing. Rehearse feeling these same feelings while you're imagining studying a subject you don't ordinarily like. Imagine yourself in that situation, in that class that you dislike and don't do well in – a chemistry class, calculus, French, whatever it is. Then imagine feeling calm and confident, enjoying being there, liking the class, enjoying the homework, feeling aggressive, being relaxed.

What you're doing is giving the mind and the nervous system a positive experience in that situation or in that class. Then the mind doesn't have only negative experiences to draw on.

Draw a circle on a clean sheet of paper and put a dot inside it. That represents one negative experience. Put in more and more dots. These represent all the bad experiences and the negative things you have imagined and said about those experiences. When the circle is filled with dots, you have very negative feelings about that subject or situation.

Now, come outside of that circle, draw another circle, and put one solitary dot in the new circle. This dot represents one positive experience you can give yourself through using your imagination. Now you've begun to move in another direction. You do it again and again. Pretty soon you've built a number of positive experiences with the imagination. Now you can draw on these instead of on the negative ones.

Back in Chapter 6, we referred to a startling discovery psychologists have made: they say that a *vividly imagined* experience is no different to the mind and the nervous sytem from a *real* one.[1] So by practicing in this way, rehearsing positive, helpful feelings, you can, in effect, become positively "experienced" without experience, through the imagination.

Self-Talk

The other aspect of the mind that you need to use consciously and positively to change your interest in a class or situation is self-talk. You approach positive self-talk in the same way you approached visualization.

List the ways you feel when you're involved in a subject or activity that you do well in. The same words may come to mind as before: calm . . . confident . . . relaxed . . . aggressive . . . focused . . . into the challenge of the situation.

Just as you turned each of these into a feeling, you can also turn each of these into a statement that you can say to yourself over and over again. The statements should be positive, in the present, as if you already possess the qualities that you want, like this:

• I feel calm, I feel confident, I feel relaxed when I work on math.

- I really enjoy math homework.

- I'm good at math. I solve the problems easily and confidently.

- I'm very aggressive about doing my math homework.

- I love math.

- I keep my focus throughout my math work and tests.

Write out a series of affirmations like this, and then say them out loud and silently in your mind. You can do relaxation beforehand, or you can just repeat these phrases. Say them often. Say them with strong feeling and intention. Say them as if you mean them.

Psycho-Cybernetics by Maxwell Maltz (New York: Pocket Books, 1969) and *What to Say When You Talk to Yourself* by Shad Helmstetter (New York: MJF Books, 1986) are good resources for more information on visualization and self-talk.

Strategy D
Reading and Math
Two Helpful Programs

Reading

A great approach to reading is outlined in Jim Trelease's *The Read-Aloud Handbook* (the newest edition is called *The New Read-Aloud Handbook*).[1] If you want a way to be positively involved in reading, you'll want this book. When our daughter was three years old, it became our "bible" for reading.

Getting children to want to read is at the heart of Trelease's handbook. He writes, "The problem is that we have concentrated exclusively on teaching the child *how* to read, and we have forgotten to teach him to *want* to read. The desire to read is not born in a child. It is planted."[2]

The Read-Aloud Handbook gives advice on everything from when to begin reading to children (as early as possible) to how to deal with the issue of television. The book also contains a list of many good read-aloud books with a short description of each.

In addition to giving convincing evidence of the advantages of reading aloud, this handbook suggests ways to make the experience effective and enjoyable, suggestions such as:

- Read aloud to your children regularly.

- Model love of reading by reading at home yourself.

- Take children to the public library often, beginning when they are toddlers.

- Discover children's interests and find books in those areas.

- Choose read-alouds *you* enjoy – it will show.

Our advice is, get this book, read it, and follow the advice in it. If you do, your children will learn to love reading. You will be rewarded many times over.

Math

Jim Trelease's conclusion about reading – "The desire to read is not born in a child. It is planted" – is equally true of mathematics. And math has a further handicap – it's not as naturally interesting for many people. When we read, whole worlds of the imagination are unlocked. For most of us, that's not true of math.

There is a program that is very helpful for "planting" the desire to do well in math – Kumon Math – and it helps with other subjects as well. The Kumon Math program started in the 1950s in Japan when Toru Kumon, a high school math teacher, began to help his second-grade son in math. Kumon created worksheets for his son, Takeshi, to teach him the basics he needed to do well in school math.

By the time he finished sixth grade, Takeshi had "completed the differential and integral calculus of the high school curriculum,"[3] and soon his father had a new occupation – providing the materials he had developed for his son to other parents. Today, Kumon Math is the largest after-school study program in the world. In 1993, "more than 1.6 million children in Japan and 350,000 children in 27 countries around the world were studying with the Kumon Educational Method." And there were "over 85,000 studying Kumon in North America."[4]

Kumon Math covers a wide range of math needs. The program begins with drawing lines and counting for preschoolers and extends through calculus and statistics. The principles of Kumon are simple:

- daily practice

- placement at the most suitable level for progress

- progress at the child's own speed

- mastery through repetition

- self-confidence through mastery

The benefits are:

- the habit of daily study

- parent involvement

- the development of independence

- the confidence that comes from competence

- mastery of math skills

One great value of Kumon for parents is that it makes positive involvement easy. Parents can do simple things like helping time the work and circling the missed problems for children to do corrections.

The Kumon company also has a reading program. Like the math program, Kumon Reading involves doing an amount of daily reading and reading-related work, answering comprehension questions, and studying vocabulary. The Kumon Reading program is like the math program in concept and organization and has many of the same qualities and benefits.

For information on Kumon Math and Reading in your area, contact a local Kumon office or at the national office:

Kumon U.S.A., Inc.
2200 Fletcher Ave.
Fort Lee, NJ 07024
tel 201-947-4475
fax 201-947-6061

Notes

Introduction

1. Jim Trelease, *The Read-Aloud Handbook* (New York: Penguin Books, 1982), p. 35.

Chapter 1. Parents Are the Key

1. William Raspberry, "Simple Things Parents Can Do," *Washington Post,* September 9, 1994.

2. Anne Henderson, *The Evidence Continues to Grow* (Columbia, Md.: National Committee for Citizens in Education, 1987), p. 1.

3. As cited in Henderson, *The Evidence Continues to Grow,* pp. 23–25.

4. Richard Riley, "An Open Letter to Parents," (Washington, D.C.: U.S. Department of Education, September 2, 1994).

5. Kathleen Cotton and William G. Savard, *Parent Involvement in Instruction, K-12* (Portland, Ore.: Northwest Regional Educational Laboratory, 1982), pp. 45–46, 75–76.

6. Faith Clark and Cecil Clark, *Hassle-Free Homework* (New York: Doubleday, 1989), p. 7.

7. Mary Jordan, "Pupils Give Their Parents 'D' for School Involvement," *Washington Post,* May 12, 1992.

8. Lori Connors and Joyce Epstein, *Taking Stock,* Report no. 25 (Baltimore, Md.: Center on Families, Communities, Schools and Children's Learning, August 1994), pp. 6, 8, 11.

9. Connors and Epstein, *Taking Stock,* p. 8.

10. As quoted in William Raspberry, "Getting Youngsters Ready to Learn," *Washington Post,* September 21, 1992.

11. Raspberry, "Simple Things."

12. Connors and Epstein, *Taking Stock,* p. 8.

Chapter 2. A Model for Positive Involvement

1. Shinichi Suzuki, *Nurtured by Love* (Athens, Ohio: Ability Development, 1983), p. 2.

2. Jim Trelease, *The Read-Aloud Handbook* (New York: Penguin Books, 1982), p. 32.

3. Kenneth Blanchard and Spencer Johnson, *The One Minute Manager* (New York: Berkley Books, 1983), pp. 80–81.

4. Blanchard and Johnson, *The One Minute Manager,* p. 81.

Chapter 3. Applying the Model to Schoolwork

1. Anne Henderson, *The Evidence Continues to Grow* (Columbia, Md.: National Committee for Citizens in Education, 1987), p. 31.

Chapter 4. Setting Goals

1. Colman McCarthy, "Good Enough Never Is," *Washington Post,* August 25, 1994.

Chapter 5. Hard Work Leads to Success

1. Jaime Escalante and Jack Dirmann, "The Jaime Escalante Math Program," *Journal of Negro Education* 59 (1990): 408.

2. Escalante and Dirmann, p. 423. To put this in perspective, the science-tech high school our daughter attended, a "recognized school of excellence" and the largest high school in Maryland, had fifty-six students take, not necessarily pass, the AP calculus exam in 1992. That was the twelfth largest total out of 10,000 high schools in the United States offering AP calculus.

3. Escalante and Dirmann, "The Jaime Escalante Math Program," p. 415.

4. Benjamin Bloom, ed., *Developing Talent in Young People* (New York: Ballantine Books, 1985), p. 3.

5. Bloom, *Developing Talent in Young People,* pp. 473.

6. Bloom, *Developing Talent in Young People,* p. 440–443.

7. Harold W. Stevenson and James W. Stigler, *The Learning Gap* (New York: Summit Books, 1992), pp. 99–106.

8. Cited in Patrick Welsh, "Classroom Potatoes," *Washington Post,* May 24, 1992.

9. Stevenson and Stigler, *The Learning Gap,* p. 95.

10. Bloom, *Developing Talent in Young People,* p. 4.

11. Bloom, *Developing Talent in Young People,* back cover.

12. Bloom, *Developing Talent in Young People,* p. 4.

13. Escalante and Dirmann, "The Jaime Escalante Math Program," p. 409.

14. Brooke A. Master, "D.C. Child Leapt from Depths of Welfare to Top of Law Class," *Washington Post,* May 17, 1992.

Chapter 6. Believing in Your Child

1. Robert Rosenthal and Lenore Jacobson, *Pygmalion in the Classroom* (New York: Holt, Rinehart & Winston, 1968), pp. 5–6.

2. Rosenthal and Jacobson, *Pygmalion in the Classroom,* pp. 175–177.

3. Rosenthal and Jacobson, *Pygmalion in the Classroom,* p. 181.

4. Jaime Escalante and Jack Dirmann, "The Jaime Escalante Math Program," *Journal of Negro Education* 59 (1990): 416.

5. In Martha C. Brown, *Schoolwise* (Los Angeles: Jeremy P. Tarcher, 1985), p. 146.

6. William Raspberry, "Expectations Work in Both Directions," *Pensacola* (Florida) *News-Journal,* July 24, 1994.

7. Raspberry, "Expectations Work in Both Directions."

8. Albert Mehrabian, *Silent Messages* (Belmont, Calif.: Wadsworth, 1971), p. 43.

9. Stephen Covey, *The Seven Habits of Highly Effective People* (New York: Simon & Schuster, 1989), pp. 19–20.

10. Maxwell Maltz, *Psycho-Cybernetics* (New York: Pocket Books, 1969), p. 32.

11. Maltz, *Psycho-Cybernetics*; Shad Helmstetter, *What to Say When You Talk to Yourself* (New York: MJF Books, 1986).

Chapter 7. Habit: The Key to Motivation

1. Lisa Leff, "Even at a Top School, the Temptation Is Just to Slide By," *Washington Post,* April 5, 1992.

2. Quoted in William Raspberry, "Revealing the Codes to Success," *Washington Post,* April 24, 1992.

3. Quoted in Leff, "Even at a Top School."

4. Jack Taylor, "Making Good Students Starts in the Home," *Pensacola* (Florida) *News-Journal,* May 31, 1992.

5. William James, *Writings 1878–1899* (New York: Literary Classics of the United States, 1992), p. 146.

6. Quoted in Stephen Covey, *The Seven Habits of Highly Effective People* (New York: Simon & Schuster, 1989), p. 46.

7. Nathan Caplan, Marcella H. Choy, and John K. Whitmore, "Indochinese Refugee Families and Academic Achievement," *Scientific American,* February 1992, p. 39.

8. Steven Waldman and Karen Springen, "Too Old, Too Fast?" *Newsweek,* November 16, 1992, pp. 80–81.

9. Robert J. Samuelson, "After-School Drag," *Washington Post,* November 11, 1992.

Chapter 8. Establishing the Homework Habit

1. Nathan Caplan, Marcella H. Choy, and John K. Whitmore, "Indochinese Refugee Families and Academic Achievement," *Scientific American,* February 1992, pp. 36–42.

2. Dan Oldenbury, "Boob Tube Brain Drain?" *Washington Post,* October 12, 1992.

3. Ina V. Mullis et al., *Report in Brief: NAEP 1992 Trends in Academic Progress,* U.S. Department of Education (Washington, D.C.: U.S. Government Printing Office, 1994).

4. Jim Trelease, *The Read-Aloud Handbook* (New York: Penguin Books, 1982), pp. 93–97, 98–100.

5. Kenneth Blanchard and Spencer Johnson, *The One Minute Manager* (New York: Berkley Books, 1983), p. 39.

Strategy A. Mnemonics: Retaining Information Easily

1. Harry Lorayne and Jerry Lucas, *The Memory Book* (New York: Ballantine Books, 1974), pp. xii–xiii.

2. Peter Russell, *The Brain Book* (New York: Hawthorn Books, 1979), p. 128.

3. Russell, *The Brain Book,* p. 128.

4. Lorayne and Lucas, *The Memory Book,* p. 22; Tony Buzan, *Use Your Perfect Memory* (New York: E. P. Dutton, 1984), pp. 52–53.

5. Russell, *The Brain Book,* p. 129.

6. Buzan, *Use Your Perfect Memory,* p. 41.

7. Quoted in Lorayne and Lucas, *The Memory Book,* p. 17.

Strategy B. Time Management: Making the Most of Study Time

1. Dale Carnegie, *How to Stop Worrying and Start Living* (New York: Simon & Schuster, 1948), pp. 183–184.

2. Marc McCutcheon, "A Proper Engine for the Soul," *Reader's Digest,* January 1993, p. 172.

3. Peter Russell, *The Brain Book* (New York: Hawthorn Books, 1979), p. 96.

4. Tony Buzan, *Use Your Perfect Memory* (New York: E. P. Dutton, 1984), pp. 222–223.

5. Buzan, *Use Your Perfect Memory,* p. 224.

6. Buzan, *Use Your Perfect Memory,* p. 225.

7. Buzan, *Use Your Perfect Memory,* p. 225.

8. Buzan, *Use Your Perfect Memory,* p. 225.

9. George Miller, "The Magical Number Seven, Plus or Minus Two," *Psychological Review* 63, no. 2 (March 1956): 81–96.

10. We read this in an account of an interview with Yo Yo Ma and spoke with the cellist's agent, who verified that this information is consistent with the kinds of stories Yo Yo Ma has told.

11. Russell, *The Brain Book,* p. 89.

12. Russell, *The Brain Book,* p. 89.

13. Russell, *The Brain Book,* p. 84.

14. Tony Buzan, *Use Both Sides of Your Brain* (New York: Plume, 1989), p. 64.

15. Buzan, *Use Both Sides of Your Brain,* p. 64.

Strategy C. Interest Management: Liking the Work You Have to Do

1. Maxwell Maltz, *Psycho-Cybernetics* (New York: Pocket Books, 1969), p. 32.

Strategy D. Reading and Math: Two Helpful Programs

1. Jim Trelease, *The New Read-Aloud Handbook, revised edition* (New York: Penguin Books, 1989).

2. Jim Trelease, *The Read-Aloud Handbook* (New York: Penguin Books, 1982), p. 24.

3. David W. Russell, *Every Child an Achiever* (New York: Intercultural Group, 1994), p. 31.

4. Russell, *Every Child an Achiever,* pp. 126–127.

Acknowledgments

There are a number of people who have offered help, advice, and support in writing this book. First, there are the readers. We would like to thank:

- Chris and Mai Avery, Beverly Chapman, Dr. Robert Coursey, and Carolyn Johnson for their reactions to earlier versions of the book.

- Helen Fournier and Dr. Harold Shinitzky for their advice on later drafts.

A special thanks to Kay Bean, who has seen and given suggestions for all the versions – a real feat of endurance and patience.

The readers gave a lot of time and attention, offering perceptive, honest advice, often in the face of resistance.

We would also like to say thank you to:

- The parents who shared stories of their work with their children, and the parents who participated in the survey.

- Jeff Ghannam who freely shared with us his enthusiasm, experience, and materials on self-publishing.

- Jenna Dixon for her cheerful, invaluable advice in seeing this book through production.

- Kristine Thompson for giving her time and expertise to designing the cover and logo.

- Ina Margaret and Woodrow Lynn for unfailing interest and support.

Finally, a thank you to our daughter, Sarah, who weathered many evenings dominated by discussions of "the book" and three years of remarks like, "Well, we should have it wrapped up by this weekend."

Index

About the Authors

Jack and Marsha Youngblood have extensive experience with teaching, parenting, learning strategies, and writing. Both hold master's degrees.

They have taught in public, private, and international schools. From 1977 to 1991, they went from suburban Maryland, to an international boarding school located at 6,500 feet in the Indian Himalayan Mountains, to three U.S. State Department schools in Saudi Arabia and Pakistan. They've worked with students and parents from many different backgrounds. They've seen schools as insiders – teachers – and as outsiders – parents. They know well what school is like for children. Between them they have taught many of the basic subjects, including English, math, social studies, computer studies, study skills, psychology, sociology, instrumental music, and drama.

Jack is director of the Achievement Center in Bowie, Maryland, where students come for tutoring, study skills, Kumon Math and Reading, and SAT preparation. At the Center, he has also advised parents looking for ways to work effectively with their children on schoolwork. He has given numerous presentations on this subject to PTAs and other organizations. During fifteen years spent working in the study skills–learning strategies area, Jack established study skills programs in two international schools and served as a consultant to three other schools. He has presented workshops at teachers' conferences in New Delhi, Lahore, Kathmandu, and Bangkok.

Marsha is program director for graduate studies in TESOL and early childhood education at Mt. Vernon College in Washington, D.C. She has developed freshman English programs for minority students at the University of California at Davis, taught English and journalism in State Department and international schools, and served as publications director for an international school. Marsha's work in English and her years editing and writing led her to develop effective strategies that break writing into a doable process for students at any grade level. Since returning to the United States, she has taught workplace literacy classes and edited or contributed articles to *Educational Leadership, READ Perspectives,* and *R & D Preview.*